Advance Praise for
Enlightened Negotiation

"Through his powerful stories, Dr. Nazari teaches you how to use negotiation to build trust and interact with family, friends, colleagues, and clients in a way that creates healthy and thoughtful relationships. *Enlightened Negotiation* is a must-read if you want to become the best in how you relate to and connect with everyone in your life."

—**Bo Eason**, former NFL standout, acclaimed Broadway playwright and performer, and Presence/Story coach

"Dr. Mehrad Nazari's *Enlightened Negotiation* provides an elegant solution for the most pressing problems of our time. This entertaining and easy-to-read guide gets to the very heart of what matters most in our world. The solution to most of our problems, both personal and global, involves collaboration and win–win outcomes. It's clear that the old model simply isn't working. Mehrad's offering is truly enlightened. Read *Enlightened Negotiation* to prosper."

—**Janet Brown**, President FundX Investment Group

"*Enlightened Negotiation* is a new, practical, and illuminating method for conscious negotiations and sustainable relationships. It is an essential guide for applying higher universal principles to our daily interactions that are embraced by enlightened leaders, entrepreneurs, and individuals. Dr. Nazari provides structured negotiation skills that you can implement immediately. His unique and diverse background makes him the most qualified to present this integrated approach. This book is destined to become a classic in its field."

—**John Mackey**, Co-Founder and Co-CEO, Whole Foods Market

"Dr. Nazari's approach elevates negotiation from the usual competing attempts to avoid leaving a dollar on the table to the more artful, cooperative process of finding mutually beneficial solutions."

—**Jacob Tanzer**, Arbitrator & Mediator, former Litigator and Justice of the Supreme Court of Oregon

"*Enlightened Negotiation* is a must read for anyone who wants to be a true collaborator. Rather than approaching every interaction with others as a win–lose battle, this book is all about making your interactions with others into collaborative, win–win relationships."

—**Ken Blanchard**, Coauthor of *The New One Minute Manager* ®
and *Collaboration Begins with You*

"*Enlightened Negotiation* prepares you to negotiate by using astute observational skills, situational awareness, and advanced planning techniques. This book gives you exactly what you need to succeed in negotiating the big game of life! It provides you the road map that leads to personal and professional success, financial security, and over all prosperity. It is truly enlightened writing."

—**Philip and Gayle Tauber**, Founders Kashi Company

"Healthy relationships, business and personal, support healthy lifestyles. Dr. Nazari's unique perspective and techniques enable the kind of compassionate and thoughtful give-and-take from which all relationships will benefit."

—**Deborah Szekely**, Founder, Golden Door Spa and
Co-Founder, Rancho La Puerta

"*Enlightened Negotiation* is a gift to everyone who is interested in approaching life and negotiations with understanding of the power of building trust and living with a higher consciousness. Negotiations are ever present in our lives, and there is now a path to creating win-win scenarios for both parties. It is a must-read!"

—**Peter Davis**, Co-Founder and CEO of IDEA Health & Fitness Association

"*Enlightened Negotiation* unpacks the fine line that many trip over between securing professional advancement while maintaining spiritual equanimity. Through his diverse experience, Dr. Nazari is uniquely qualified to dispel these myths that habitually create conflicts in the "winner" or "loser" paradigm. This structured approach brings wholistic awareness to our intentions and interactions while successfully informing the decision-making process.

This is an indispensable navigation guide touching all aspects of our life."

—**Richard and Leslie Morgenthal**, Founders Morgenthal Frederics

Enlightened
Negotiation

Enlightened Negotiation

8 Universal Laws to Connect, Create, and Prosper

Mehrad Nazari, PhD, MBA

SelectBooks, Inc.
New York

This edition published by SelectBooks, Inc.
For information address SelectBooks, Inc., New York, New York.

First Edition

ISBN 978-1-59079-368-1

Library of Congress Cataloging-in-Publication Data
Names: Nazari, Mehrad.
Title: Enlightened negotiation : 8 universal laws to connect, create, and
  prosper / Mehrad Nazari, PhD, MBA.
Description: First Edition. | New York : SelectBooks, Inc., 2016. | Includes
  bibliographical references and index.
Identifiers: LCCN 2015032888 | ISBN 9781590793688 (pbk. : alk. paper)
Subjects: LCSH: Negotiation in business.
Classification: LCC HD58.6 .N323 2016 | DDC 302.3--dc23 LC record available
at http://lccn.loc.gov/2015032888

Book design by Janice Benight

Manufactured in the United States of America
10 9 8 7 6 5 4 3 2 1

To my Teachers,
past, present, and future

Contents

Acknowledgments

This book has a life of its own. It is the culmination of the work of so many along the way, and I am honored to know them. They all have been essential parts of my life.

First I thank my wife, friend, partner, and soulmate, Michele Hébert, for her support, encouragement, love, spiritual connectedness, and humor; and I thank her parents, Bill and Olive.

When my literary agent Bill Gladstone wrote, "This is a book whose time has come," I reflected on all those who have been supportive on my path in developing the Enlightened Negotiation philosophy. My profound gratitude to Bill Gladstone for understanding the essence and the message of this book and finding the perfect home for it, SelectBooks: Kenzi, Nancy, and Kenichi Sugihara's eyes for detail sharpened my message. I am so grateful for what they do and who they are.

Perhaps I could use the word *mentor* for those who guided me along the way, but the Sanskrit word *guru* says it all: *dispeller of darkness*. Those who shed light on this path. My academic guru, the late professor Frederick Dow, was a true mentor and a great source of encouragement to me for developing a negotiation course at US International University. We all have that one teacher who always stood out, the one who lifted us. For some this person is an elementary or high school teacher; mine showed up during graduate school. Dr. Dow was that academic guru for me.

My spiritual guru, Walt Baptiste, showed me the inner light, put me on my spiritual path and taught me balance—the laser sharp edge between strength and softness, materiality and spirituality. And my gratitude to his wife, Magana, for her joyful spirit and her way of always reminding me of my real essence. My heartfelt appreciation to my revered spiritual teacher, Swami Veda Bharati, for his intellectual vigor, wisdom, and gentleness. He was the embodiment of love and showed me the way of the heart. And to the Zen master Kyozan Joshu Roshi for his lifelong teaching and instilling discipline in me with our eighteen hours of meditation day after day. Even though none of them are in this plane, their teachings and influences are ever so alive. Then, when I was not searching, my professional guru, Bo Eason and his amazing wife, Dawn, showed up in my life to infuse energy in my mission to spread the message of this book—a first draft ex-NFL player, playwright, and the greatest speaker of our time. Namaste to all my gurus.

My sincere thanks to Arlene Matthews, my developmental editor, who took my academic writings and gave them structure for the book with a generous heart and continued support; and to Dennis Mathis, my editor, who softened the tone of book and made the proposal read so perfectly.

My profound gratitude to Phillip and Gayle Tauber, Richard and Leslie Morgenthal, Jacob and Elaine Tanzer, Peter and Kathie Davis, and Tan Sri Datuk Dr. Mohan Swami for their friendship and continued support as well as their valuable contribution of the case studies and stories in this book. They all embody the essence of this book by being successful business and civil leaders with deep spiritual connections. All of you make our world a much better place; thank you!

Our mentors in life show up clothed in many different ways. At the height of my business career, where a doctorate degree was not a factor in my business success, Dr. Tomer Anbar was that mentor who showed up as my lifelong friend. He pushed me and kicked me to pursue my degree and did not take no for an answer. Special thanks to Robert Caplan from whom I have learned so much and whose friendship I treasure, alongside the friendship of his dear wife, Dr. Carol Randolph.

It is a blessing to have angels around you to uplift and be there for you, like Terry Gopadze, Stephen Sorkin, Victoria Danzig, Dr. Alan Nahan, Betty Rauch, Linda Wertheimer, and Rhana and Jim Kozak. My life has been so much richer because of having friends like Christine Forester, Rob Quigley, Kathleen Hallahan, Harvey Berger, Janice Mulligan, Bill Brooks, John Holtz, Roger Mora and the late Lewis Weinberg.

My admiration and appreciation goes to the Esalen family, Michael Murphy, Dr. Gordon Wheeler, Nancy Lunney-Wheeler, Cheryl Fraenzl, and the rest of the staff who have created the perfect environment for the exploration and acceleration of human potential. My deep gratitude to my Rancho La Puerta family: Sarah Livia Brightwood, my spiritual sister; and Deborah Szekely for her visionary character; the late Alex Szekely, who carried the helm; Roberto Arjona, Alex Von Bidder, Phyllis Pilgrim, Victoria Larrea, and the rest of the Rancho La Puerta family for providing a place to connect to our inner source.

My sincere acknowledgment to those whom my academic life would have not been enriched without their help: Dr. Gary Hayes and Dr. Mink Stavenga, who believed in my developing the International Business Negotiation course at USIU, and to my colleagues and all my students that brought so much energy and character to make the negotiation courses outstanding experiences. Thank you! Of course none of these would have been possible if it were not for the inspiration and knowledge that I received from their lifelong pursuit of understanding human interaction and negotiation: Dr. John Nash, Abraham Maslow, Dr. Carl Roger, Dr. Daniel Kahneman, Roger Fisher, and Dr. Bill Ury, thank you.

Enlightened Negotiation has been enriched by the creative work of Braid Creative who understood my philosophy and transformed it into images and narratives.

Of course, I give my loving thanks to my parents, Minoo and Mohammad, and my siblings, Mitra, Mercedeh, and Mahdad; and to my nephews and nieces who brought so much joy to my life: Houman, Brigitta, Cyrus, Celeste, Chloe and Shahrad, Barbara, Soraya, India and Kambiz, Thais, Delara, Layla, Dalia and Jalil.

Last but not least, my heartfelt gratitude to all those who participated in my courses, seminars, and workshops, and, of course, to you, the reader. Together we will be able to create a community of enlightened negotiators to elevate human interactions and make the world what it ought to be and could be. Thank you!

Introduction

Let us begin anew, remembering on both sides that civility is not a sign of weakness. Sincerity is not always subject to proof. Let us never negotiate out of fear. But let us never fear to negotiate.[1]—John F. Kennedy

My father was 81 when I visited him overseas after not having seen him for a few years. He was a retired civil servant with a great deal of interest in philosophy and poetry. Although he did not have a college degree, he was intellectual by nature and surrounded himself with philosophers and poets. He took delight in the fact that I had received my doctorate and was now teaching at a university.

He had learned, too, about my interest in mindfulness practices and meditation, and he was prepared to engage me in some intellectual sparring on the subject.

One afternoon he asked me, "So what is this mindfulness and meditation thing?"

I told him, "Dad, it's something you have to experience for yourself. I can't explain it."

He rolled his eyes and walked away.

The following year when I visited him, he asked me the same question. I told him, "Dad, it's not something you can intellectualize; it's a matter of direct experience. Are you sure you wouldn't want to try it for yourself?"

This time I felt some disappointment when my father again walked away.

My next visit was when my father was 84.

This time he succumbed to my insistence that mindfulness and meditation were subjects that needed to be experienced, not talked about. He agreed to give them a try.

To start him on his way, I decided to share with him a simple breathing practice called "the three-part breath." You start by lying down and mindfully inhaling first into the lower abdomen, then adding the diaphragm, and finally the upper chest. At the same time, you focus on exhaling from those parts of the body, but in the reverse sequence: chest, diaphragm, and then abdomen. This is a wonderful way of introducing the concept of mindfulness, because it's a simple practice that, somewhat like patting your head while rubbing your belly, requires a surprising amount of concentration. It also slows the breath down and induces a sense of calm alertness.

After fifteen minutes I asked my dad to rise up to a seated pose. It was hard for me to gauge his reaction at first, but then I realized tears were flowing down his cheeks.

Rarely had I seen my dad's tears. And never so clearly.

There was a long pause.

"Nobody ever told me how to breathe before," he said.

Breathing was something he'd done for over eighty years, every moment of his life, but he had never connected deeply with his breath. The expression on his face was priceless—it was as if he had been cheated of this pleasure all those years!

We all breathe, but very few have been taught how to do it properly.

Likewise, we all negotiate every day, in the give-and-take of occupying the world along with other people. But very few of us have been taught how to negotiate mindfully.

As you read these sentences, bring your attention to your breath. How are you breathing? Without changing anything, ask yourself: Am I breathing efficiently? Am I using my lungs and diaphragm to their fullest extent?

Although we breathe constantly, unless we happen to be a professional singer or a wind-instrument player, yoga practitioner, or perhaps a woman taught how to breathe in preparation for childbirth, it's unlikely we'll ever be trained in breathing techniques.

Similarly, we negotiate all the time—far more frequently than we realize—but we rarely take the time to fine-tune our skills as negotiators. As oxygen-dependent beings, we must breath in order to survive. But let's not forget that we are social animals dependent on the help of others, and as social beings we are also bound to cooperate, as well as compete, just to stay alive.

Generally we think of negotiation in terms of making business deals or conducting a transaction or reaching a settlement, such as bartering at a flea market or trying to talk our way out of a traffic ticket. But we're also negotiating when we interact with our spouse, children, neighbors, relatives, friends, or adversaries. We work out agreements and promises in countless little ways with our colleagues—employer or employees, our teachers and students, our customers and creditors. We also belong to groups that negotiate with one another. Even when we're not directly involved, our representatives are negotiating on our behalf with other communities, other nations.

Why is it that we don't take the time to fine-tune our skills in breathing and in negotiation? We came into the world, and with one smack we started pumping air; the ability to breathe comes to us involuntarily. Perhaps this is why we accept whatever pattern we fall into as equally involuntary—something that is just *there*. As babies, when we needed food we cried; it worked well to get everyone's attention. Then caresses and nourishment followed, and in this way our hunger and other needs were taken care of. It seems as if our first experiences establish for the rest of our lives how we negotiate to get what we want.

In the same way, our methods for interacting with others are shaped by our earliest successes and failures. As toddlers we soon discover a less draining alternative to kicking and screaming to get what we want—we turn on the charm. Smiles, laughter, and excited giggles (or the threat of a frown) prove to be so useful that older children become adept at imitating adorable infants, a skill that can last well into adulthood. One way or another, childhood trial-and-error experiences shape much of whatever skill in bargaining and compromising we have as adults. Even representatives of sovereign nations, in tense negotiations in moments of global crisis, have been known to act like big babies.

For so many people, a personal style of charming one's way through conflict, or withdrawing and playing hard to get, or raging and pounding on the table, is simply what they've brought with them from the nursery to the conference room. But just as being attentive to the natural cycles of our physical breathing pattern can guide our mental awareness into a more efficient rhythm, we also have the power to modulate and enhance our ingrained negotiating style, which will affect the way we think of give-and-take situations generally.

Being mindful of what we are doing as we negotiate teaches us new ways of finding our way forward toward agreement, and each success will lead a step at a time toward business progress, future opportunities, and more harmonious and productive personal relationships.

Twenty-three years ago, I had a rude awakening to what much of the business world considers negotiation. Having completed my PhD program, I was teaching a graduate course in negotiation. To expand my understanding of where the best teaching practices in the field of negotiation stood, I enrolled in as many courses and seminars as I could afford, familiarizing myself with different points of view and lecturing methods. I traveled all over the country and sampled the styles of many different teachers.

In 1992 I attended a two-day course and workshop given by a renowned consultant on negotiation with an impressive list of clients. The lecturer started the session by hammering us with "rules" and tales of his own many successes in bullying people: "Never accept the first offer! Never!". . . "Act as if the offer is insulting!" . . . "Then I tore up the offer right then and there—and immediately nailed them for five percent more!"

I was sitting patiently waiting for some punch line, but there wasn't one. Instead, listening to him was like being punched in my stomach.

I looked around the audience for some clue as to what I was missing. Everybody seemed to be robotically attentive, taking copious notes on everything the instructor shouted and pounded at them. I knew many of the attendees were there at the expense of their employers and were grateful they'd been given the special privilege of attending this "advanced course" in a valuable skill.

The longer I listened, the more I became convinced that everything I was hearing amounted to gamesmanship and chicanery. I wanted to get up and walk out of the room, but my optimistic side kept repeating: *Mehrad, don't be too judgmental. Wait a bit longer. Stay open-minded. Maybe he's saying this hogwash to make a point.*

Toward the end of the morning session, I was still listening to the instructor proclaim in his growling voice yet another list of "elements" for successful negotiation: "Always make it a win-win negotiation" and "Towards the end, it's okay to throw your opponent a bone! Make them happy!"

That did it for me. When the morning session ended, I collected my handouts and caught the instructor as he was leaving.

I politely said, "I have to leave. This just isn't the right course for me. My idea of negotiation is very different. I'd like my tuition refunded."

He immediately put on his "negotiator" mask and gruffly dismissed my request: "Hey, you can't go to a restaurant, eat some of the meal, and walk away without paying. There's no refund, my friend. You might as well stay for the rest of it."

I'd been ready to walk out of *his* dinner since the appetizers were served, and I'd stayed this long only because I thought he deserved a fair hearing. It was clear this was not the "advanced *negotiation* course" for me. I'd wasted a morning, but I wasn't wasting my money.

I decided not make a scene and walked away without entering into negotiations with this man under his terms. But a few weeks later I reminded him that a professional reputation also has value and that I was a colleague in his field. I got my full tuition back.

When I look back at the experience, I remember my shock as I looked around the audience. It was as if I were watching a group of intelligent people mindlessly drinking poisoned Kool-Aid because a charismatic charlatan bullied them into it. This man was planting and promoting very harmful ideas.

That day I had met my nemeses: people who teach haggling instead of negotiation. I felt a responsibility to help undo the damage such self-styled experts were capable of causing.

Since that day, I've devoted myself to teaching and promoting principled negotiation in the classroom and in the boardroom. At the same time, I have been on a mission to discover the natural and universal laws governing our interactions and negotiations. This quest has taken me on spiritual pilgrimages to meet and learn from Hindu scholars and Zen masters.

What I will be sharing with you in this book is the culmination of two decades of my journey—one foot on the trail of business, professional, and material life and the other foot on the spiritual trail.

To demonstrate and awaken the genius within us, we must master the art of collaboration: co-creation in the spirit of oneness, dignity, and fairness. By bridging the worlds of materiality (business and money), governance (personal, family, community, and global), and spirituality (actualization of our authentic self), Enlightened Negotiation capitalizes on our spiritual essence, inner wisdom, and authentic values in business and governance to help us enjoy a meaningful life experience. It also presents business principles that are equally important in spiritual organizations in order to create a sustainable spiritual entity for lasting guidance.

When we consider what's at stake in negotiations going on at every moment—in corporate boardrooms, parliaments and congresses, international trade conferences, and institutions trying to end tensions and bloodshed—how can we deny that negotiation ought to be a spiritual practice? Enlightened Negotiation enables us to understand spirituality as being in the wakeful state of oneness. In this state our interactions, negotiations, exchanges, and trades are the embodiment of our higher humanity where we experience values like truth, fairness, growth, compassion, goodness, love, and connectedness. In this state we receive guidance through our intuition and insight and we channel those strengths so the creativity will flow through us and become a catalyst for harmony and prosperity.

1

The Law of Trust

Trust is to human relationships what faith is to gospel living. It is the beginning place, the foundation upon which more can be built. Where trust is, love can flourish.[2]—Barbara Smith

A PERSONAL EXPERIENCE OF NEGOTIATION

I was eight years old, living in Tehran, Iran, when I first dreamed of starting my own business, and I set out to launch my entrepreneurial venture the next summer, as soon as school was out. My vision of exactly how all of this was going to happen was clear. At an age when American children traditionally set up lemonade stands, I had something much more serious in mind: retailing toys throughout my neighborhood of Tehran. Although my father was an important civil servant (in effect, one of the five "mayors" of the complex and busy city), he did not have a head for business, and money was a constant tension in our home.

The consumer side of the toy market was a field in which I had considerable expertise; I knew my demographic (the kids on my block) and precisely which products would catch their eyes. My start-up capital was the savings I'd painstaking accumulated for much of my life. I had worked out the details so clearly in my mind that I saw no way the enterprise could fail. I was absolutely convinced I would soon make my first fortune and provide my parents and siblings with a life of comfort and security.

The instant I announced to my parents that I was starting a business, my mother told me I would be doing no such thing. Set up a stand in front of the house to sell trinkets to strangers? It was one step above begging! "There are better ways for you to spend your time off from school," she told me, "than learning to be a street peddler."

My father was at least curious enough to consider my prospectus, but it was clear he wasn't going to contradict my mother.

Throughout the rest of the school year, I applied myself to intense negotiations with my mother toward achieving my goal—getting her "green light" so my business plan could go forward. I was elated when my efforts yielded a breakthrough preliminary agreement: If I gave in to all Mom's demands, she "might think about it."

I did my homework, kept my bedtime, did extra chores around the house, and was always available for last-minute runs to the market at odd hours. Keeping up with Mom's demands became more time-consuming than I had anticipated, but my laser-sharp focus on my plan and all the sacrifices I was enduring (I lost no opportunity to make Mom aware of just how much I was suffering) ultimately softened her heart, and she approved my plan with only a list of restrictions, regulations, and laws punishable by death-by-homework governing my business hours of operation and geographical boundaries. She also attached a list of books she expected me to read by the end of the summer.

The world was a glorious place the day I went to the wholesale market to select my initial inventory. The excitement and joy of finally moving toward my goal translated into a sense of determination and fierce independence as I walked the aisles among my fellow merchants.

The next morning, although our neighborhood was a quiet place, the fanfare of my grand opening was as loud as a circus parade inside my head. There was no question that my wooden-crate stand, with the gleaming toys arranged strategically on a background of fabric my sister loaned me, was up to par with the department store windows downtown.

Opening day was a smashing success. Sales volume was strong, and neighborhood support was enthusiastic at both my morning and afternoon sessions. (From lunch until three, I had to stay at home, working through Mom's reading list.) That night, I proudly counted my money and stacked it where I could look at it as I fell asleep.

The next morning I couldn't wait to run out of the house and get on with business. The morning sales were so strong and I was so excited, I pushed the envelope of the time I was required to have my afternoon break by getting to my stand early and setting out new items in preparation for the brisk business to come.

A man—a grown-up riding a bike—came along and began checking out my wares. For an adult, he showed a lot of interest in toys. He would pick one up and say, "Oh, wouldn't my son have fun with this," and then, "My little girl would love this one." He collected in his arms quite a few items he thought his children would enjoy. I was so thrilled to have a major sale taking shape that I beamed with pride when the man asked if I'd consider a package deal on everything he had in his arms. I had already given a few discounts to kids on the block who weren't as blessed with financial success as I, but this man was asking for a much larger discount since, as he pointed out, he was buying up most of my inventory!

While we bargained, he handed me a high-denomination bill, and he kept proposing new figures as I fumbled to count my available coins and bills, worried I'd lose the sale if I couldn't make change. Then he offered to give me smaller currency instead, which made me start adding and subtracting all over again. This happened a few times as he kept bargaining and changing his mind and selecting new items. In addition, he asked for a bag for all the items he'd purchased, so I had to scramble around under the counter to find one.

With a satisfied smile he said goodbye and jumped on his bike. I was in heaven as I started to rearrange my display, filling in the gaps where so many items were now gone. I kept thinking about the man's children, how lucky they were to have such a good father, how happy they would be when he got home, all thanks to my vision of a toy store . . .

As these happy thoughts were going through my mind, I opened my cash box and was bewildered to see only a few coins. Where was all the paper money the man had passed through my hands so many times? Did I put anything in my pockets, or drop a wad of bills? I looked everywhere, but the money was nowhere to be found. It was gone! The bike man had taken it all when I wasn't looking. He had cleaned me out! He had stolen my money! He had stolen my dream! Didn't he know how hard I had worked the whole year?

I tried with all my might to block from my mind what had happened, as if everything would be reversed if I could only fool myself as thoroughly as he had fooled me. But always the facts came rushing back. I felt the ground melt beneath me as everything I thought I could rely on had dissolved like cotton candy into a sticky nothing.

How could he do it? A grown-up! Someone's *father!*

My dream in tatters, I rearranged my few sad remaining toys on the shabby display cloth. My stand now seemed so empty, lifeless, soulless. My yearlong dream twisted into a nightmare as I gathered my things and hung out my "Closed" sign.

People on the street looked different to me now, with something sinister in their smiles. Beneath the surface, was everyone like the man on the bike, waiting to take all I had the instant I turned my back? What about all those grown-ups, friends, and neighbors, who over the next days encouraged me to keep following my dream? Maybe it was my duty to tell all nice people the dark truth and warn them about evil people cruising around our neighborhood like sharks on bicycles. But how would I be able to tell good people from the sharks? How do you know who to trust?

That day I learned the first law of negotiation, The Law of Trust.

TRUST: THE FOUNDATION OF A RELATIONSHIP

A towering house of cards can be an intriguingly beautiful construction. Building such a structure, defying gravity card by card, requires planning, precision, patience, and attention to detail. But all it takes is one shaky move for such a precarious edifice to collapse. The same is true of an elaborate sand castle—a lot of creativity that melts away with the next tide.

Real castles and houses require, first of all, secure and durable foundations. Conducting a masterful negotiation and crafting a mutually satisfying agreement are great achievements, but what good is all that effort if the outcome, the manifestation of our intentions, is built upon an unreliable foundation? If there's no assurance of follow-through, an otherwise perfect negotiation can be a waste of creative energy.

Trust is the foundation of any agreement. Confidence that the other party will keep its commitments provides both parties with the assurance necessary to keep moving forward productively even though many tough issues remain to be worked out. When either party's commitment to its promises is perceived as doubtful, a marriage, a business arrangement, or even a multinational peace treaty can fall apart in an instant because there's no solid foundation of trust to build upon.

Perception of reliability is not just an important factor in whether a negotiation's outcome will be a lasting success. A sense of trust is critical in shaping an environment of positivity and mutual support that helps the parties aspire toward excellence and endure frustrations along the path to an agreement.

In an environment devoid of trust, uncertainty creeps in and can spread like a toxin. In such a situation, an assumption that the pieces will fall into place at the right time is replaced by an implicit—sometimes explicit—threat: "If X fails to happen, Y will result." In personal relationships as well as business ventures, a threatening atmosphere replaces faith with fear and decisiveness with hesitancy, diminishing productivity and opportunities for progress.

Trust vs. Mistrust

Trust yourself, then you will know how to live.[3]

—Johann Wolfgang von Goethe

What is trust? In the broadest terms, it's assured reliance on the character, ability, strength, or truth of someone or something.

The practical definition of *trust* in the process of negotiation is a mutual perception of congruity of words and actions. Put simply, we expect the other party's deeds to live up to their words, just as we expect others to "consider it done" when we give our word. We come to trust others when we've seen evidence of how well they carry out their promises, just as we must demonstrate to others our trustworthiness.

The antonyms of trust—distrust, mistrust, doubt, uncertainty, unreliability—are also enlightening. If we think of the apex of trust in a relationship to be like the peak of a mountain, anything less is like wandering in the gloomy shadows of a deep valley. At the peak, our view takes in expansive fields of opportunities; in the valley we're cramped and limited.

The basic concept of negotiation is that each party is committing to provide certain actions or items based on the confidence—call it belief or faith if you prefer—that something else will be delivered by the other party at some point in the future. A classic example is the "short sale" in financial markets, where it's perfectly acceptable for a trader to sell something he has yet to buy, an arrangement that speeds trading and creates liquidity.

The degree of trust (or distrust) sets and modulates the quality of what can be accomplished speedily as well as the potential for growth as the relationship expands.

Is Some Doubt Inevitable?

The concept of our oneness with all beings is a fundamental tenet of almost all wisdom traditions, and fully embracing this awareness would allow us to fully trust one another. In a meeting of "enlightened beings" there would be no reason to be guarded or anxious about being harmed, cheated, blind-sided, or attacked. The energy we ordinarily devote to staking out and defending our boundaries would be available for more productive and positive purposes.

In an enlightened environment, there is an underlying element of trust and hope. One assumes wisdom and intelligence will prevail, and all parties will work in unison within a frame of well-justified hope.

In the material world as distinct from the aspirational one, there exists things like suspicion, fear, and mistrust that are triggered by an evolutionary survival mechanism that keeps us wary of dangers in a hostile environment.

All animals, including human beings, react to possible threats to their well-being or survival with abrupt bodily changes as every resource is put on alert. It's debatable whether a crocodile experiences fear just as humans do, but humans respond to perceived threat just as most animals do, as a rush of alertness prepares us to choose among running away, hiding, or striking out at someone. Fear is unpleasant, but it equips us with a vivid preview of the worst that *can* happen. To disregard our fear would be to place ourselves in potential mortal jeopardy. Our evolved physiological defenses predispose us to visualize all sorts of actual and potential threats, even those that exist only as dark phantoms in our imagination.

Fear is useful in more ways than one. Niccolò Machiavelli wrote in *The Prince* in 1511, "Since love and fear can hardly exist together, if we must choose between them, it is far safer to be feared than loved."

The force of fear is a motivating factor in many aspects of everyday individual and social behavior. Machiavelli's principle has been put to abundant use in politics and marketing for centuries. Frightening people in order to get them to do something or even buy something has become such a common practice that we often don't recognize it. Why wouldn't it be? People are motivated to protect themselves and minimize risk; a good scare triggers their receptivity to any suggestion of a way out of danger. If our goal is Enlightened Negotiation, however, activating another person's self-defense barriers merely to gain an advantage has the disadvantage of closing us off to more positive possibilities.

Think about the body language of *trust*. It often takes the form of an open-arm gesture, signaling a welcoming attitude offering promise and potential. On the other hand, *mistrust* growing from a perception of threat forces us inward, hunching and embracing ourselves, a closed-off "go away" posture that constrains our actions, restricts our thoughts, and narrows our vision.

To Trust or Not to Trust?

Trust, but verify![4]—Ronald Reagan

In many cultures and societies, trust forms the connecting threads in a web of relationships. Members of a group sharing a bond of trust can trade and negotiate efficiently on the basis of reliable underlying assumptions. Within many tight-knit social groups, a person's word is as good as any written document. A foundation of mutual trust expedites agreements and transactions, and the energy that would otherwise have gone into structuring ironclad protections and threatening counter-incentives can then be available for more productive purposes.

Over time, even business relationships established out of expediency, when parties have no option but to trust each other, can grow to greater levels of trust to have a broader and deeper foundation for good relationships.

In the early 1990s I was active as a real estate investment advisor in San Diego. Real estate is a field in which, typically, people make the largest investments of their lives. At that level of personal risk, the element of trust is of utmost importance. Aware of this, I always made sure my clients understood that if I presented an opportunity to them, it was something I had personally examined fully and would consider investing in myself. It was always clear to me their confidence in the property's value was directly tied to their trust in me as a person who does his homework and keeps his word.

One day I opened a letter from a client and was surprised to find in it a check for $300,000 made out to me personally. Attached to it was a note:

Mehrad, please invest this money in the next real estate investment opportunity you find suitable for me. My wife and I will be traveling and not easy to reach. Thanks. Harry.

Although I had worked with Harry in the past, I'd had no forewarning that he would be putting hundreds of thousands of dollars in my hands to spend for him as I thought best! I sat back in my desk chair somewhat in shock, overwhelmed not so much by the sizable responsibility Harry's check had placed on me (I was confident I could find a suitable property for him) as the depth of his trust in me the note represented.

Trust seldom appears out of the blue the instant we meet someone. It needs time to grow and take root. In many cross-cultural negotiations, or indeed in any negotiation outside of one's prequalified circle of trust, there is often a testing process the parties must pass in order to establish a basis of trust before moving on to substantive issues.

Many cultures have a kind of ritual or "dance" before negotiations begin in earnest, a process of getting to know the other party, adjusting to their energy and rhythm, and measuring their trustworthiness. It's easier to notice the trust-building rituals of other cultures than to be aware of our own. Americans, for example, take pride in a "let's get down to business" directness, and can be impatient or misled when a counterpart from another culture is slow to get to the issues at hand. In the Far East, the Middle East, and in Latin countries, for example, it's common to have a period of social interactions like dining together during which it's impolite to discuss business deals—an enjoyable courtship, in effect, while everyone takes a good look before they leap. There's sound logic for the "socialization delay" built into the customs of such cultures. Among other things, a go-slow period is seen as a preventive practice. It's easier, less costly, and certainly more pleasant to have an unhurried get-to-know-you process at the outset, the reasoning goes, than to fix something after promises have been broken.

American-style directness can sometimes lead to problems a more leisurely pace might avoid. We have a tendency to leap *before* we look, entering into agreements before confirming the reliability of the other side or establishing a solid common ground of understanding and trust. Fortunately, Americans also have an extensive (and expensive) judicial system to resolve the problems resulting from our frequent leaps of faith.

Fast-paced American culture has its own trust-forming rituals, of course, even if they're as offhand as arranging to meet for coffee. Just by showing up at the agreed-upon time and bringing along a promised document, we pass reliability tests. By taking the time to talk about something other than business and exchange common courtesies, we plant seeds of trust that will take root and deepen, given time.

Although it would be convenient to do business only with an inner circle we trust intimately, it's not very practical (and definitely not good for business expansion) to limit our interactions to a circumscribed sphere of minimal risk and uncertainty, whether it's our neighborhood or nation. In real life, situations arise in which the uncertainties include negotiating with others we don't fully trust.

At the beginning of my own career in real estate, I too frequently limited myself to doing business only with those I trusted, and I avoided getting involved with anyone not in my close circle of associates or I had some question about. Rejecting people is easier than accepting people, and in those years I fell into the habit of judging people and rejecting opportunities.

It's possible my childhood experience of failing at business because of a crook caused me to think narrowly and be suspicious of others as an adult, but my youth in Tehran only reinforced the tendency. There is an old Persian saying: *A person who's bitten by a snake will be afraid of a black and white rope.* Much of what I learned in business school in that era was about survival: *It is a jungle out there. Only the fittest survive. It's a dog-eat-dog life.*

The fear of establishing a business relationship with a stranger I couldn't yet fully trust eventually hampered my business development. I had a small circle of people I regularly represented who, like me, valued longtime relationships with strong bonds of loyalty. But it was a limited environment, and the nature of business requires expanding the number of one's clients.

I had only an off and on switch for trusting people and allowing them into my circle. Anyone with even with a minor incongruity between their words and actions was immediately crossed off my list.

It is true, unfortunately, that there are people in the world skilled at exploiting the confidence others place in them ("con men" for short) who prey on their victims' need to trust and be trusted. The "pigeon drop" is a classic example of a scam in which the perpetrator preys on the eagerness of the *mark* or *pigeon* to demonstrate his own trustworthiness by putting down a deposit to secure a stake in a much larger easy-money payoff—which never materializes, of course, because the scammer makes off with the security deposit, leaving the pigeon with nothing but a determination to never trust anyone again. Obviously none of us wants to be a pigeon.

The Dimmer Principle

The question of whether anyone can be trusted had haunted me since my encounter with the man on the bike. The answer came to me in a flash one day. Such moments of clarity are signified in cartoons as a lightbulb going on over a person's head, and in this case the image is particularly apt.

I was overseeing one of my fixer-upper remodeling projects. In this project, in addition to improving basic items such as flooring and appliances, we were updating all of the overhead electrical fixtures and the wall switches. I had to choose between installing economical on–off switches or more expensive dimmer controls. Though it would add somewhat to the cost of the project, the decision was obvious to me. It was clear to me having a range of choices would be far preferable to only on–off. If I to were live there, wouldn't I want the dimmers?

In my quest for self-improvement, both personal and professional (I always consider myself a work in progress or in need of upgrading), my epiphany came when I realized there was a useful analogy here, a connection between home improvement and personal improvement. My life would be improved if I took out all the either-or situations and replaced them with a range of many choices. This would certainly include the issue of trust that still plagued me, wouldn't it?

Suddenly I had my answer to the question of how I can know who to trust: Trust shouldn't be an all-or-nothing proposition, a choice between all-out commitment and cutting someone off entirely. People like the bike man represent one end of the spectrum, but just about everyone else is trustworthy *up to a point*. If we think of our willingness to trust another person as a dimmer switch, we can then modulate the mix between assuming everything will work out just as the person says and building in safeguards just in case it doesn't.

From that moment on, I experienced a greater openness toward my contacts and clients, a willingness to listen to proposals and agree to move forward creatively *up to a point*. At that stage it's then appropriate to verify whether promises have been kept.

In practical application, it's always best to balance trust with verifications. As we prove our trustworthiness, trust can be extended and there's less need for verification in the next step forward.

Sources of Trust

He who does not trust enough will not be trusted.[5]—Lao Tzu

As human beings, we like to think of ourselves as the only creatures with a highly developed moral code guiding our behavior, but in fact we see animals behaving virtuously all the time, sometimes in astonishingly loving and self-sacrificing ways. Is it truly our moral sense that restrains our worst behavior, directs us to do the right thing, and enables us to form trusting relationships beyond our immediate families? Might there not also be a biological component that influences how, when, and indeed whether we "take the high road" of trust and trustworthiness?

In his 2012 book *The Moral Molecule*, Dr. Paul Zak,[6] Director of Neuroeconomics Studies at Claremont Graduate University, explains how his research revealed the role of the hormone oxytocin in human behaviors we associate with concepts such as morality, empathy, and altruism. Oxytocin originally was known to be a hormone produced during physical bonding experiences such as childbirth and breast-feeding in women, and during sexual intimacy for both sexes. Studies indicated people's level of trust increases if they simply inhale oxytocin molecules. The substance increases generosity, too, increasing "donations to charity" in laboratory simulations by 48 percent.[7]

Dr. Zak's findings further reveal that when people *feel trusted*, there's a similar rush of oxytocin in their brains and bloodstreams. As a result of that surge, they become measurably more generous and protective, behavior that inclines others to extend their trust. In other words, even at a mechanistic biological level, the process of trusting others and receiving their trust in return creates a virtuous circle of pleasurable positive reinforcement, expanding outward like rings from a pebble dropped into a pond, engendering empathy and bonding between individuals and enabling us to deeply connect with, nurture, and aid others.

But what if a person is among the five percent of the population that has a natural oxytocin deficit? In such individuals, what else might account for our predisposition to trust and be trustworthy? What else might account for differing capacities among individuals to extend trust to others? If the answer is not wholly biological or socio-economic, we might consider the spiritual perspective.

In each of us, the Unadulterated Self is trustworthy and trusting. The nature of our true and authentic Self is love, unity, and harmony. It's certainly true our natural inclination to trust may be deformed by conditioning that keeps us on guard against people who are indeed capable of exploiting and betraying trust, perhaps because we've been on the receiving end of actual betrayals in our past experience. If we are aware of such conditioning, however, we can at least prevent it from irrationally coloring all of our interactions—for instance, with those we have no verifiable reason to doubt.

It is a conscious choice whether to behave out of our authentic and natural inclination to trust or to give in to distrustful impulses streaming from reactive states of mind. The former can be nurtured and sustained with practice, developing the habit of reaching within to connect with one's True Self, where we can count on nature to provide a wellspring of confidence that supports us in our quest for people we can trust fully. If, on the other hand, we habitually answer to the misguided impulses of a mind conditioned to fear and distrust, we limit our natural potential and stunt our ability to take advantage of the universe of possibilities available to us as our birthright.

Ultimately, the issue of trust reflects back on us as individuals, to the choices we make. Beyond the question of "Can I trust her?" we must also ask, "Can she trust me?" Am I trustworthy? Would I trust someone like me? Trustworthiness must be cultivated and nurtured so that we may keep our intention pure and authentic, and we must remember that trustworthiness is a quality of the self that can be measured only by others.

In the course of developing another of my real estate projects, I received a call from my sales representative, who told me he needed my help in advising a family who had been eager to purchase the last condo unit in our project. The couple loved the unit, but for some reason they hesitated to "pull the trigger" on the transaction. The rep asked if I could meet with them.

I met the family at the condo. After introducing myself, I asked frankly about the couple's concerns underlying their hesitation. They told me they loved the unit . . . apart from one detail. They were concerned about its lack of natural light.

When I'd arrived, all the lights in the unit were on, which was customary. I impulsively walked through every room turning off all the lights. Then I turned to the couple and asked, "How does it feel with only natural light?"

Instead of doing what some real estate salespeople are trained to do—highlight the positive features of a property (in this case, well planned and modern artificial lighting), thereby masking a potential drawback as long as possible—my impulsive choice was to confront the situation head-on. I intended to openly demonstrate to the couple that my willingness to look at the situation through their eyes was sincere, and that I genuinely understood their own impulse to suspect the sales rep might be hiding something.

I was open about myself as well, presenting myself not as a salesman but as an advisor worthy of their trust, making it clear to the couple that my intention was *not* to sell them a home they wouldn't feel comfortable living in.

We stood for a moment, letting our eyes adjust to the change. Eventually the wife broke the silence by admitting that the natural light was actually more pleasant than she had expected; she said she hadn't appreciated the view from the windows before. It was a grudging admission, yet I sensed that something important in her perception had changed.

There is a second part to this story that might seem like a detour from our discussion of the topic of trust, but it demonstrates a concept known as "universal support." Sometimes, if we are open to a spiritual point of view, we have the undeniable sense that the universe is actively conspiring with us—somehow whirling planets and galaxies align to help us achieve worthy goals.

Here's what happened: When I'd finished turning off all the lights, I walked to the center of the living room where the couple was waiting with their children. The wife had just admitted the unit wasn't quite as gloomy as she feared. Just at that moment, rays of late afternoon sunlight fell upon the windows of the room, and the condo lit up with a brilliant, golden sunset. The effect could not have been better timed and executed if I had hired a team of Hollywood lighting technicians. It was, at that moment, a miracle. We stood bathed in warm sunlight, taking in views of the rest of the apartment along the hallway. The children raced off to view the effect from "their" rooms, and before the sun had fully set, the couple had instructed me to draw up the necessary paperwork.

This little miracle reminds me of what Steve Jobs once said:

> You can't connect the dots looking forward; you can only connect them looking backwards. You have to trust that the dots will somehow connect in your future. You have to trust in something—your gut, destiny, life, karma, whatever. This approach has never let me down, and it has made all the difference in my life.[8]

HOW TO ESTABLISH TRUST

Establishing trust takes time. In many negotiations you do not have the luxury of time; so if you need a fast track approach, these are the four elements for creating trust:

- The authenticity is the foundation upon which you can build trust. Be truthful to yourself and to others.
- Understand and speak the nuances of their language, slang, terminology, and jargon. That means knowing their culture, environment challenges, and opportunities.

- Emphasize the importance of your relationship with them and the inter-dependent nature of your relationship.
- Offer the concession before they ask AND make sure to emphasize the value and importance of it.

Trust, Your Moral Credit Rating

It takes 20 years to build a reputation and five minutes to ruin it.
If you think about that you'll do things differently.[9]
—Warren Buffet

Adam Smith, best known for his 1776 book *The Wealth of Nations*, a founding document of modern economics, was a moral philosopher and a pioneer in the field of political economy. In his earlier 1759 book, *The Theory of Moral Sentiment*, Smith suggested that what we think of as moral conscience arises from social relationships. He elaborates on a theory of sympathy in which the act of observing others makes people aware of their own moral behavior. We share the joy and pain of other people, Adam Smith explained, so we behave in ways that promote joy and avoid pain.

It's clear we're predisposed to trust when we feel comparatively stable and comfortable in our own lives. New research goes beyond this, indicating that people living in richer, more egalitarian countries are more likely to trust their fellow human beings than people in poorer, less egalitarian countries that are not as trusting. But here too we have an asterisk: The United States is an exception. In 2008 the United States was ranked the 10th least trusting country in the world,[10] with only 45 percent of Americans agreeing with the statement "most people can be trusted."[11] (Gallup Poll 2005). According to Edelman Trust Barometer, in 2009 people's trust in US business fell to 38 percent, the lowest level since records have been kept.

Generally speaking, people are drawn toward a personal or business relationship with you if (A) they *like* you (as a person, company, product, brand, mission, or philosophy) and (B) they *trust* you. Basically this boils down to a matter of competence and delivery. *We* have what *they* need, and we are able to deliver in a way they can count on.

Reputations are earned through a track record of competence and performance. Henry Ford once said, "You can't build a reputation on what you're going to do." Trust represents the accumulated scores we've received, over a span of the past, in fulfilling our promises. Reputation is our scorecard, our batting average. It captures in shorthand the "permanent record" of a complex living person, but it should not be mistaken for the person himself. As Abraham Lincoln said, "Character is like a tree, and reputation like a shadow. The shadow is what we think of it; the tree is the real thing."

Any bank or merchant who extends credit to a customer would want to review the person's credit score. Based on that pattern of past performance, the lender then determines whether to offer, or decline to offer, credit. Personal and professional relationships are also evaluated according to similar but less quantifiable scoring systems.

Recall that, according to Dr. Zak's research, five percent of us do not have the typical hormonal output related to natural bonding and trust-building experiences. For these individuals, the absence of normal oxytocin levels means their capacity for compassion and empathy might be weak or nonexistent, signaling a possible disability when it comes to fully, authentically participating in the natural process of being accepted as a trustworthy and reliable individual and being able to trust others. It's another way of saying nature imposes limits on what we can assume, and we must recognize that signals of good-faith intentions are not sufficient in themselves to ensure a mutually trusting relationship with everyone we encounter. Science confirms what we know from age-old lore as well as direct personal experience: We must stay alert to the fact that not everyone is by nature trustworthy; there's always the possibility of "a wolf in sheep's clothing."

An often told parable describes a scorpion and frog who meet on the bank of a river they both want to cross. The scorpion asks the frog to carry him on his back across the river.

The frog says, "But you're a scorpion! How do I know you won't sting me to death if I help you?"

The scorpion tells him with a perfectly rational attitude, "Sting you? Then we would both drown. Why would I do that?"

The frog, satisfied with the scorpion's undeniable logic, invites the scorpion to hop on his back and starts to swim across the river.

Midstream, the frog feels a painful sting, and he's soon struggling against the onset of paralysis as he fights against the river's current. The frog realizes neither he nor his passenger will make it to the opposite shore.

With his last breath the frog asks the scorpion, "*Why?* Why did you do sting me, when you promised you wouldn't? Now we're both going to drown!"

The scorpion shrugs and replies, "That's my nature."

Intangible and Rippling Effects of Trust

The deal ends but the reputation lasts. The emission admission scandal of VW is a real example of this. VW, short for Volkswagen, or "peoples' car," went into full production after WWII and quickly became one of the best-selling cars in history. In early 2015, VW surpassed Toyota as the best-selling automobile manufacturer. This carefully cultivated brand, with a long standing history of reliability, lost its reputation after the Environment Protection Agency in September of 2015 charged the automaker with purposefully installing software in some VW diesel vehicles to cheat environmental regulations.

Volkswagen's CEO, Martin Winterkorn, a longtime company insider and the highest-paid CEO in Germany, had to resign in the wake of this scandal. The cost to the company is expected to exceed the $7 billion originally estimated. Company stocks had already plummeted 23 percent.[12] Why? Because of the Trust factor.

The Volkswagen issue was so significant that the German Engineering Federation, which represents machinery makers and is closely intertwined with the auto industry, said there was a risk that the "Made in Germany" brand could suffer. The organization said in a statement that it was worried "that one instance of misconduct could be carried over to all of German industry."[13]

Because VW tried to cheat on environmental regulations, the rest of the German industries may suffer because consumer trust in the German brands has been compromised after this scandal. This is the intangible and rippling affect in negotiation. In this case it is a negative one.

CYBER TRUST

In the past few decades, a new environment has emerged in which trust is a critical component. Not only is your reputation on the line, it's also *online*.

The Internet, social media, and smart phones have made possible new forms of human interconnectedness at a scale never before imagined. It's now possible for any of us to participate in a market that dwarfs the scale of the largest "brick and mortar" institutions imaginable. It is called *collaborative consumption*, where participants trade in goods and services that existed previously, but that were never traded on such mass scale. In this virtual market, participants can share, swap, rent, barter, or trade with millions of other individuals in vast online communities.

A good example is Airbnb, an online service that provides a platform for "hosts" to rent unoccupied living space and other "bed and breakfast" style short-term lodging for out of town visitors. As of November 2012, Airbnb had over a quarter of a million listings in 30,000 cities and 192 countries.

Similar online communities exist for people seeking to rent their cars (WhipCar), share their bikes (SpinLister) or office space (ShareDesk), or even their pets (DogVacay). LendingClub is a remarkable online resource for those seeking financing and loans for start-up businesses, a lively alternative to traditional lending institutions. The players in this new market are countless "micro-preneurs" who can now put their assets to work supporting worthy startups that conventional financing arrangements tend to overlook or undervalue, on an individual-case basis or through investment pools.

These global—but ironically intimate—forms of interaction are a fresh take on traditional lending institutions that have become abstracted, over the centuries, from their origins in simple human connectedness. Participants in the digital marketplace have found new ways to accomplish the fundamental objectives of wanting to connect to, communicate with, and creatively share ideas with others—even perfect strangers. Much of the new technology serves simply to extend what we do naturally, and despite the sophisticated algorithms and business models, often it all comes down to digitizing a fundamental quality our ancestors would easily recognize: personal reputation.

Just as credit ratings serve as a measure of "good risk" in traditional banking, emerging online institutions rely on personal recommendations in the form of consumer or seller ratings, analysis of correlated online behavior, or other measures to evaluate the essential trustworthiness of individual people involved in the vast exchange.

To have a chance to thrive in this new environment, a person must earn the trust of others by consistently displaying reliability and basic character values. The feedback received must be positive and transparent. Every good review turns up the dial a notch on the potential buyer's reliability rating, but even one negative review casts a cloud of uncertainty.

TRUST, ONCE BROKEN, IS VERY DIFFICULT TO REPAIR

"Win as Much as You Can" is an exercise often used in negotiation training sessions. As the title suggests, it's a game that helps participants consider what "winning" actually means in a group context.

Players are divided to groups of four. Players are to choose an X or a Y without communicating with each other and, depending on the players' choice, there is payoff at the end of each round. The game is similar to rock-paper-scissors: Each choice has value only when compared with what the other groups choose.

Only before rounds 5, 8, and 10 are players given a chance to confer with each other and perhaps work out a strategy. On these rounds the bonus rewards are multiplied by 3, 5, or 10 respectively.

The catch is that the scoring system incentivizes betraying the group decision, such as choosing X when you were expected to choose Y.

Many elements of real-life negotiation are illustrated in this game. It's fascinating to watch as participants run up against complex concepts, such as cooperation versus competition, credibility and trust, or joint gain as opposed to individual gain, and how these elements are affecting individual decision-making process.

A major lesson from the game is the so-called "social trap," in which long-term success requires voluntary mutual trust, whereas short-term gains are possible by breaking the bond of trust. The danger of a self-centered and shortsighted decision is frequently evident, and casual competitors can quickly devolve into cutthroat adversaries. Although many of the elements mentioned above are learned behaviors, there are some concepts like trust that are deeply rooted in the individual characters of the participants. Sometimes a hidden side of a person spills out in the heat of competition.

I first participated in the game at the National Marketing Institute in Chicago many years ago. One of my teammates, also from San Diego, was a pleasant man who became more and more determined to win as much as he could as the game progressed, and he favored the betrayal strategy. Watching his decision-making process, I found myself in a dark mood, as if I were being robbed in broad daylight. He reminded me of the man on the bike who stole the money from my toy-selling venture!

It wasn't much of a surprise, more than twenty years later, when I noticed this fellow's name in the newspaper and read that he had been forced from the office he'd held as a high-profile civil servant. The unsettling experience of watching him in the win-all-you-can simulation came back to me. Clearly, that day we played the game he failed to learn the lesson that betraying trust might be profitable in the short run, but sooner or later there's a reckoning.

Once it is broken, repairing trust can be extremely difficult, if not impossible; there will always be a shadow of doubt. Building trust takes a long time. Rebuilding it takes forever.

Trust is at the core of all personal relationships. It has an organic and dynamic quality, ebbing and flowing as events put it to the test. A solid foundation of trust and reliability fuels us with hope and confidence, propelling our positive attributes toward ever-higher levels. If trust is missing, doubt, dread, and despair rush in to fill the void.

As physical human beings, we are a bundle of feelings, aspirations, desires, and sometimes fears. We walk around like water balloons, a flood of emotions barely contained within a fragile skin. At the slightest contact with a hard edge, the balloon can rupture and all that anxiety and emotion will come pouring out. Trust betrayed is often that hard edge.

Trust is the tree from which we expect to harvest the fruit of our negotiations. If sprouting branches are damaged, the tree can still heal itself and bear fruit. If the root is damaged, however, healing is likely to be lengthy and imperfect, and there's a chance the tree will be fruitless and eventually wither away.

The opposite of trust, confidence, and security is the feeling of a constant awareness of threat. There is fear of an opponent having a siege mentality bent on tense competition or in the worst-case scenario, pre-emptive-strike warfare or revenge.

We must make absolutely certain there is no miscommunication or misunderstanding before we question another's trustworthiness. When another person's commitments seem questionable, it's still possible to sensitively discuss the details and work out a resolution, as long as there's an underlying perception of authenticity and sincerity backed by a history of trustworthy performances.

If it's our own trustworthiness in question, we must evaluate the congruity of our own words and actions, reflect on our track record for meeting our commitments, be careful of making promises we'd be hard-pressed to keep, and be aware of the lasting damage to our reputation that a single default of our responsibility can cause. If something we weren't aware of has been seeding distrust and threatening our reputation, we should act quickly to clarify the facts. When our authenticity is being measured, we need to be aware of the impressions we make on others, and we should be quick in clarifying misperceptions.

SUMMARIZING THE LAW OF TRUST

- Trust is the foundation of any relationship.
- The fruits of our negotiation may be immediate, but our reputation and the trust we earn will last beyond the end of a deal.
- Trust is a moral credit rating.
- Use the dimmer principle in modulating your trust in relationships.
- Once trust is broken, it is very hard to repair.

2

The Law of Intention

If you don't know which port you're sailing to, no wind can help you.[14]—Lucius Annaeus Seneca

THE SPIRIT AND THE TECHNIQUE

In a tale of ancient Persia, a young man nearing the end of his apprenticeship in the shop of a master potter has ambitions of starting his own business. Day after day for twelve years, the apprentice has watched his master at work, kneading the clay to a perfect consistency before sitting down at his wheel. The young man observed every nuance: how the master sprinkled water on the wheel before he set the clay upon it; how he started the wheel slowly while his fingers grazed the surface with the lightest touch; the way he closed his eyes as his hands tightened on the clay. By now, the movements of the master's fingers were like a dance the apprentice knew by heart. Apprentice and master had worked side by side like two oxen in yoke, stacking firewood in the kiln, loading each pot carefully in its proper place in the kiln, and keeping watch during the long firing. Together they opened the kiln the next day and arranged the pottery on the shelves of the shop.

There was one step of the process the apprentice knew he would not imitate in his own shop. Before applying the glaze, the old master would hold each pot close to his face and *talk* to it while turning it fully around. Only then would the old man set about applying the glaze with patient concentration. The apprentice promised himself he would not waste time with an old man's strange habits.

The apprentice soon opened his own shop, despite the master's warning that there was still much for him to learn. He built himself a kiln just like the old man's and carefully followed his teacher's formula step-by-step.

But, firing after firing, pieces that went into the kiln perfect in every way came out of the oven with crackled glaze. Customers noticed the imperfections at once and laughed at the young man's asking price; in the end, he settled for pennies just to clear his shelves so he could try again. But it was to no avail. Nothing he tried kept the fine glaze from cracking.

Soon the apprentice was forced to close his shop. With his head down like a shamed dog, he went back to his master to ask forgiveness for his false pride and ignorance.

He found the master talking lovingly to a heavy milk pitcher.

"And what woman will pour from you, my beauty?" the old man was saying, turning the piece in his hands as he held it close to his eyes. "A fine, strong woman with big hands, I think, and an appetite for ripe purple plums. Oh, and a bad temper—she squawks like a blackbird."

At that moment, the old man turned and noticed the apprentice. "I was wondering when you'd be back," he said to the young man. "Take off your coat; there's a load of wood to be chopped."

"You're not the first, you know," the master said as the apprentice set about his old duties. "I've seen many students learn the techniques until they can do them in their sleep, and then they convince themselves they've become master potters. But it takes many more years to learn the *spirit* of the work. That's why your training is called *foot-o-fan*: spirit and technique. To be a skilled potter you must master both the technique and the spirit of your work. Technical skill alone is worthless.

"Did you ever notice that I talk to my pots before I put on the glaze? *A crazy old man talking to lumps of clay*, you probably thought. What you didn't notice was that, as I talk, my breath blows the fine dust off the surface and adds a bit of moisture to help the glaze adhere.

"Talk lovingly to your pots, wrap them in your spirit, and the glaze will never crack in the kiln," the old man said, dipping his brush into a plum-colored glaze.

As we begin to talk about Enlightened Negotiation, it's important to keep in mind that no two situations are identical. Every negotiation has unique elements that must be integrated into the process to realize an optimal outcome. These Universal Laws guide us to attain our full potential in our negotiations with mindfulness and higher awareness. In doing so we may achieve solutions that are worthy of evolved human beings.

Enlightened Negotiation transcends merely applying smart techniques of negotiation in order to get a bargain. It takes place only once we are attuned to our genuine desires and act consciously, choosing the proper tool for each situation. To make the best of an opportunity, we must not only be equipped with practiced skills, but also be prepared to breathe our spirit into the process.

PUT YOUR ATTENTION ON YOUR INTENTION

A good intention clothes itself with sudden power.[15]
—Ralph Waldo Emerson

A conscious action requires a clear intention. Before embarking on any journey you must know your precise current location, have a clear idea of your destination, and then plan a route.

Picture yourself on a hilltop looking across a vista of broad plains, rolling hills, and snowcapped mountains in the distance. Your chosen destination is beyond one of those peaks up ahead; you can almost see it from here.

Imagine turning yourself through the entire 360-degree view. In every new negotiation, we have the potential to move in any direction. There may be one direct route to our goal, the shortest distance as the crow flies. There are also many more meandering, but less difficult paths. Some involve intermediate goals, stages along the route to our eventual goal. Some might require us to detour away from the compass heading of our destination, and there's also the potential of wandering far away from our goal, even in the opposite direction, if we lose our fix on our goal.

You create out of your thoughts. All of man's accomplishments originate with thought. Humans had witnessed round rocks tumbling down hillsides for tens of thousands of years before someone absorbed in thinking about the problem of moving things efficiently saw a rolling rock and made a purposeful connection, inventing the wheel.

Intention is concentrated thought aimed at a goal. Research findings[16] have confirmed what most of us know from experience: Having an intention in mind while performing a task leads to a more productive result than when the same task is preformed absentmindedly. What's more, CT scans of brain activity display very different patterns depending on whether the task is performed with or without a mindful intention.

In negotiation, it is critical to keep your attention on your intention. When you are engaged in a negotiation, it is essential to keep in mind the underlying purpose.

Consider a particularly thorny negotiating situation most of us have encountered: getting an obstinate child to do what we want him to do (for his own good) without losing face or teaching the wrong lesson.

If you're a parent telling your child, "It's time to go to your room," what is your ultimate purpose, at a deeper layer, than simply placing a child in a room? Is it to instill discipline? Establish trust? Teach a lesson? Nurture growth? Are you indicating, with scientific detachment, a previously agreed-upon bedtime? Or are you once-and-for-all punishing the child so he'll be scared of you from this time on, and you'll always get your way?

Your underlying purpose will come through in your tone of voice (nurturing, robotic, or dictatorial) when you say, "Go to your room."

The child will perceive it, even if you insist you don't, and it's likely to imprint on his memory, bearing fruit far into the future. Therefore, it's wise to clarify your intention in your mind *before* you speak.

The same principle applies on the macro scale. If you are a nation having a border dispute with a neighboring country, what is the underlying objective? Is it to wreak destruction, once and for all, on a cruel and eternally despised enemy? Or is it something less drastic, a matter of the land in question being of cultural significance or potential economic value? Or is your crusade primarily a matter of a principle, of sovereignty, of recognition? Or merely a buildup of "keep your dog off my grass" tensions neighbors often experience, where cooler tempers have a good chance of negotiating a peaceful outcome?

To embark on a negotiation without an intention or goal is to walk away with a result that is inefficient at best and could be disastrous—physically, financially, and emotionally. It's a waste of resources, for one thing. The process of negotiation is time-consuming and the outcome can be taxing; therefore it is crucial that we weigh our assets, our time, human resources, and material goods before embarking on a voyage *without a clear destination* that risks the loss of everything.

A lack of clarity of intention often has emotional outcomes most of us are familiar with: buyer's remorse, seller's remorse, the misery of being at a new job and feeling ill-suited, or even perhaps the longing to dissolve a marriage before the ink on the marriage certificate has dried.

In this chapter we look at the larger perspective and potential, so that in chapter four, when we focus on the individual's needs, we may have an idea of where to meet in that larger landscape.

WHAT DOES "NEGOTIATION" MEAN?

What does the word *negotiation* bring to your mind? At the outset of a situation requiring "negotiation," what kind of emotions and expectations do you conjure up?

The term has vastly different meanings depending on cultural connotations and personal associations. To some, it evokes a hostile scene, a winner-takes-all wrestling match. To others, it might simply connote an opportunity for applying leveraging techniques for personal gain. And then there are those who look on negotiation as an opportunity for cooperation and harmonious endeavor toward mutual fulfillment.

Before examining The Law of Intention, the subject of this chapter, let's look at this complex word: *negotiation*. The exercise of clarifying it might help us appreciate the challenges we have ahead of us, as well as offer some clues to overcome them—especially since language must bridge vastly diverse cultures like those of 21st century America.

The English word *negotiation* can mean "to deal or bargain with others, as in the preparation of a treaty or contract or in preliminaries to a business deal." But it can also mean "to move through, around, or over in a satisfactory manner" or "to maneuver a difficult dance step without tripping" or "to navigate sharp curves."

In the original Latin, *negōtitāus* denoted trade or business. It was a compound of *neg* (not) and *ōtium* (leisure). In other words, *negotiation* means "that which is not leisure."

Picture yourself lolling on a canvas chair on a tropical beach with an iced tea in your hand. Now picture everything that is *not* that. *That*, according to the Roman Legion and its legacy, the Romance languages of Europe, is *negotiation*. Negotiation is no day at the beach. It *is* a constant part of our lives.

In many non-Romance languages there are no words for *negotiation* as it is used in English. Since our melting pot of American culture comprises people of many backgrounds, it should be no surprise that misunderstandings abound of what the word *negotiation* means and what its practice involves.

In the Chinese, Japanese, Arabic, Farsi, and Turkish languages, the closest approximation to the English word *negotiation* means discussion and debate, generally with no presumption of agreement. For instance in Arabic (*mufawadat*), in Farsi (*mozakereh*), and in Turkish (*muzakere*) the most applicable translation connotes a discussion, recitation, or even praise. These words, quite evidently, would apply in an amicable atmosphere suitable for disputation of high social, moral, and ethical issues.[17]

On the other hand, the words *musawama, chane zadan,* and *pazarlik* (you might recognize the root word *bazaar*) connote bargaining, bartering, haggling—or as they say in the Farsi of ancient Persia (now Iran): *mo'ameleh bazaari*, the bargaining style of the bazaar. It should be noted that a "bazaar" is a vast market where one can buy anything . . . anything! It connotes low status, street values, and petty or aggressive haggling.

Even with modern-day insight into the complex language of negotiation, even as late as 1996 the Israeli-Syrian peace talks,[18] despite a very clear mutual understanding of interests and possible solutions, were bogged down by a language gap that forestalled agreement. Why did the Syrians adamantly object to the use of the word *normalization* but accede to the term *normal peaceful relations*? And why, in the Arab world, is it an insult when Israel uses a term that could be translated as "bargaining" in the context of peace and war, life and death?

YOUR OWN NEGOTIATION STYLE

Every moment in life is a crossroad. Our decision at every step is either a move toward our ultimate goal or away from it, a credit or discredit. Is our action based on a conscious, informed, and rational choice? Is it aligned with our true intention? Or is it based simply in laziness and habit, and laden with unconscious past assumptions?

What about you? Do you haggle or discuss? How would you describe your own style of negotiation? Are you hard or soft? Do you lead or do you follow?

Let's take a look at a hypothetical situation in which negotiation takes place, an extension of the parent-versus-child scenario described above. Try to observe your own impulses. This might help you determine your own typical style of negotiation. What is your instinctive, natural reaction? You might consciously and purposefully choose any of the behavioral options listed below, or you might choose a default response out of habit, laziness, misinformation, or lack of information. Just try to be honest about what your gut response is likely to be. Make a mental note of that reaction as well as your own likely (hypothetical) course of action.

You're likely to find it enlightening to witness how everyday behavioral choices are replicated in business and corporate environments, as well as in international negotiations of global significance.

☼

A few years ago I went on an extended-family ski trip to Mammoth Mountain ski resort in California. One afternoon, knowing my wife and I would be hosting a birthday party for my sister that evening, I excused myself from the crowd of aunts and cousins and assorted children to go back to our cabin and rest. As I was leaving, my nine-year-old niece, Jasmine, rushed over to me to ask if she could come along. By the time we got to the car, her eleven-year-old brother, David, had also decided to join us.

Back at the cabin, I lay down on the couch to read my newspaper and fall asleep. Before long, I was awakened by a loud bang. Toppling from the couch in confusion, I could hear Jasmine screaming, "That's mine, that's mine!" I found her running after David, who was rushing up and down the stairs and jumping over the couch to evade her. He was yelling, "I found it first! It's mine!"

After taking a few breaths, gathering a glimpse of data, and assessing the situation, I realized that they were fighting over *the last orange in the pantry*. To say the least, I was not happy. From my point of view, I had done them a favor by agreeing to bring them back to the cabin with me, and they were now interrupting my nap with a cacophony of screaming and tattle-talking, which did not appear to be coming to an end anytime soon.

In a situation like this, what would *you* do? What is *your* first impulse?

I've shared this story with thousands of people throughout my teaching career, and I've received many different answers. The most common are:

- Ignore them completely. Do nothing.

- Eat the orange and send the children to their rooms.
- Toss a coin to see who will get the orange.
- Cut the orange in half and give half to each.
- Determine why they want the orange.
- Determine who found the orange first.
- Ask them to sit down and come up with a solution.
- Buy more oranges.

Yes, perhaps these are all valid options under the right circumstances. However, for us as Enlightened Negotiators, expectations are higher, and the course of our actions must not only be logically justified, but also resonate with our true essence. This is where The Law of Intention comes into play: We assess the situation in general, we orient ourselves as to where we are now, and then we consciously aim for a goal.

NEGOTIATION COMPASS

Negotiation is an expedition through a landscape of human interactions to discover potential meeting places where we can come together in harmony.

Our *intention* can be superimposed on this map, on our journey to work with our counterpart who will help us along our chosen route.

Determining where we will meet involves two driving forces compelling us forward: the dynamic arrow of each individual's intentions and the magnetic pull of our universal potential or calling.

Visualize again that 360-degree vista of plains and mountaintops to see where you stand now and where you want to be. Your ultimate goal, not quite visible, is beyond the farthest mountain. In your imagination, rise up into the sky and look down at your position on the terrain.

Now visualize the direct path toward your goal *intersecting with someone else's direct route toward their own goal.* For the sake of simplicity, let's visualize the other person's desired route as being at right angles to your own path toward your goal.

A Four-Quadrant Diagram of Our Negotiation Possibilities

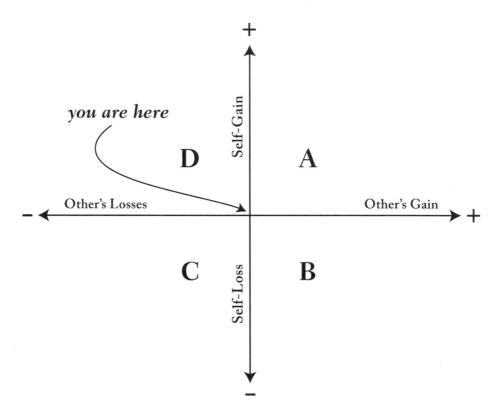

In this graphic representation of an abstract negotiation (pre-sented here for the first time, to the best of my knowledge) we will sometimes explore the negative options as well as the positive-point-ing vectors of mutually beneficial outcomes, in order to get a complete perspective on all possibilities.

The initial point of contact is where we meet "you are here," the vertical vector represents our gain/loss status and the horizontal line is our counter part(s)'s gain/loss position. Any meeting place above the horizontal line indicates our gain and below the horizontal line is our loss. Similarly the horizontal vector is our counterpart status, whereas to the right is the positive territory for them and the left is negative or loss.

Since most negotiations seek to maximize beneficial outcomes for both parties, for the sake of simplicity we are most interested in the upper-right quadrant "A" of this mapping of negotiation. (This is the only quadrant that up to now has been the focus of most behavioral analysis.) However, when necessary we'll refer to the complete map of potential behavior and demonstrate how misguided choices may lead us to negative results. The other three quadrants B, C, and D cover these negative territories.

Diagram of Quadrant A: the Mutual-Gain Territory

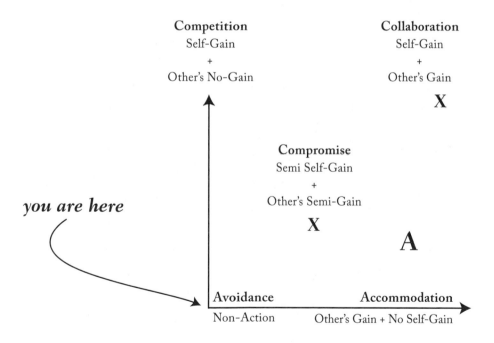

Competition
Self-Gain
+
Other's No-Gain

Collaboration
Self-Gain
+
Other's Gain

X

Compromise
Semi Self-Gain
+
Other's Semi-Gain

X

A

you are here

Avoidance
Non-Action

Accommodation
Other's Gain + No Self-Gain

Option One:
Avoidance, Denial, Non-Action

Non-action is an action of its own. The initial point of contact represents a situation that needs to be addressed and we have 360 degree options to move, but we stay put or simply ignore the situation. In our story of Jasmine and David, one action I could take would be to simply ignore their dispute as though it weren't happening. I would probably have to forget about taking a nap, my intention, while I let them fight it out and perhaps even harm each other, which wouldn't be a very positive learning experience. Stay put at the point of initial contact, "you are here." At best neither side gains or at worst both sides fall into the "C" quadrant of lose-lose territory. Nonetheless, doing nothing has the virtue of not intentionally making things worse. That is why the fear of making things worse keeps us from taking actions. Burying my face in the pillow and hoping for the best certainly is, in that sense, a valid choice—one we frequently apply to unpleasant situations we face.

Why would we choose the option of doing nothing? In our daily interactions we frequently encounter annoying situations that affect us, yet we don't bother to address them. A neighbor's dog frequently barks in the middle of the night, interrupting our sleep or disturbing our peace, but we don't do anything about it. An employee shows up just a bit late and disturbs our meetings in progress, but we don't make an issue of it. A customer is habitually behind in payment, costing us interest and annoying paperwork, but we choose to say nothing.

Any of these choices could be very well justified; we could make a legitimate case for it based on our intention and our ultimate goal.

The reasons we choose the non-action option could be:

- I don't have the time.
- It's not my responsibility.
- It will take care of itself over time.
- It's not a big deal.

- I don't like confrontation.
- It's easier to shrug it off, let it go.
- I have more important things on my mind.
- Someone else will probably fix it.
- I'm not the policeman of the world, constantly monitoring and correcting everyone's behavior.

What are the results of our choice?

The downside of doing nothing is that there are unintentional consequences. Like a boat crossing a lake against a headwind, unless someone paddles forward, things tend to drift back into one of the other quadrants where no one is getting ahead.

In the case of our story, there's bound to be resentment on one side or the other, if not both. I could easily be left with a negative impression of my sister's kids, that they have no respect for me, or for an adult's decision to rest and have a quiet time. I might well feel that agreeing to bring them back to the cabin was a mistake.

From Jasmine and David's separate points of view, they could easily feel resentment that I'm only sitting there watching while a great injustice unfolds, when I have the power to intervene and rule who gets the orange. *My uncle, who pretends to be so affectionate, doesn't even care about my being victimized. Now I see who he really is!*

This is a delayed-reaction, lose–lose scenario shown in the diagram as the quadrant C. Although we haven't *done* anything negative at the time, the residual effect will surface later. Similar resentments could easily unfold in our other examples of doing nothing. For instance, when you pass on the street the neighbor whose dog kept you awake, you're reluctant to return his smile, so he walks away thinking you're a grouch, having no idea you're suffering from lack of sleep because of his dog, or the next time the employee who always shows up late for meetings asks you for flexibility in his vacation time, and you decide not to allow any changes. Or the customer who always pays late gets crossed off the mailing list for a new promotional discount you're offering.

The Law of Intention recognizes that it's prudent, when urgent action it is not required and if we do not have a clear intention, to do nothing. The safest option is very often inaction. But it is not always a productive one, and can often generate misunderstandings.

We've all said it: *Oh that wasn't my intention . . . I didn't mean to communicate that . . . I didn't mean to give you that impression . . .* These statements of regret are very often the fruits of doing nothing positive.

Option Two: Accommodation, Concession, Sacrifice, Surrender

Another common response from those who have heard the story is: *Why not go and buy more oranges so everyone would be happy?*

This would be an act of accommodation, but it might also be described as sacrifice or concession or even surrender. Which is a "gain" for the other side and at best simply neutral or "no-gain" in our side or at worst a "loss" for us that takes us to the lose-win "B" quadrant. In our negotiation, the party giving in to the desires of the other party would be me: I'd give up my resting time and instead have to walk to the market for more oranges, while the children will, in effect, be rewarded for running around screaming.

It's important to keep in mind that the loss in a lose-win outcome can range from a minor inconvenience with no gain to a major set-back or loss. Although the words *concession, surrender,* and *sacrifice* all mean that one party benefits more than the other, they're emotionally loaded terms, and the labels we attach to an outcome can color how we value it. Being accommodating is a virtue, and giving of oneself often has beneficial effects down the road. If we think of a self-sacrificing gesture in those terms, we're likely to feel we haven't sacrificed much. On the other hand, if we think of every concession as *surrender,* we're likely to come out of a negotiation with the very outcome we feared—the loss of everything.

In spiritual terms, as much as we strive, act, and use our power to move toward our goal, it's equally essential to embrace the fact of the here-and-now, this unique moment, and let go of expectations. The true value of an outcome might only become evident with the passage of time.

For us to grow and to foster growth in others and realize our true nature, we must acknowledge that each decision or action has its own time and place. For the wheel of life to be in motion, as with riding a bicycle, once we exert our power by pushing the pedal down, we must then let go and wait for the pedal to come back up before we can push it down again. In many cultures this concept of reciprocity, of expecting the eventual return in another form of what we have given away, is embedded in the fabric of society.

In my International Business Negotiation classes, a Thai student once brought up her frustration with her American classmates and friends who immediately say "Thank you" after receiving a gift or a favor, but then never reciprocate. The Thai culture is very generous and openhearted, yet there is a limit to how often you're expected to give, give, and give. Once, when traveling in Kerala, India, I asked our host how one says "Thank you" in their local dialect. She told me there is no such word or gesture. She was surprised when I then asked how people show appreciation for what they've received. After she'd thought about it for a moment, she said, "By their actions." She explained that giving is an obligation of being a part of family or community. There's no reason to say anything about what's simply expected, although you are expected to give after you have received.

Why do we sometimes choose a self-sacrificing option during our daily interactions in our society? We do it when we help a disabled stranger crossing a street, even though it might make us late for a date. We stay late at the office to cover for a colleague who couldn't make it to work, even though we're not feeling well ourselves. We sacrifice our own interests when we let a customer purchase an order at cost, even though sales have not been good during that month. Why do we opt for accommodation outcomes? Familiar reasons include:

- It's easier for me to give up something and move on.

- I don't want to jeopardize our relationship.
- It saves time.
- The other party is going to win anyway.
- You win some, you lose some.
- There's no other option.

What are the ramifications of selecting the self-sacrificing option? Once again we must take into account the nature of our intention: Is the source of our decision conscious intent or simply laziness or habit? Any of the reasons we've listed could very well be justified, and a strong, legitimate case could be made for them. It's important, however, to keep in mind that a self-sacrificing gesture could establish an expectation in the other party's mind that we will give way in future interactions. In our story about the orange, accommodating Jasmine and David might be interpreted as approval of their wild behavior, teaching them that acting hysterical will always succeed in getting my attention. Similarly, the co-worker we covered for one time might get the idea it's okay to skip work because it gets done "automatically." The client you gave an at-cost price to might assume you have a way of remaining in business without making a profit.

Being accommodating and allowing others' interests to take precedence over one's own falls in a partially positive quadrant of our diagram "A" when simply there is no self-gain. However, if taken to an extreme, it can result in a self-loss, self-depriving or self-defeating outcome for the sake of the other party and will fall into the lose-win quadrant "B." There are, of course, exceptions; no one would question the self-sacrifice of a parent to save a child, or of firefighters and police who risk their lives in the line of duty, or an extreme situation of hunger strike to force the other party for change of action or self-immolation by a Tibetan monk with a higher goal of preserving a land and culture. But in the ordinary course of events, if others become accustomed to profiting at our expense, the cost to us could easily outweigh the benefit to others and not be sustainable in the long run.

Option Three: Competition, Assertiveness, Aggressiveness, Dominance

Among the options suggested by students who have heard my story of Jasmine and David and the orange, one is frequently suggested with a mischievous smile: Grab the orange, eat it yourself, and tell the kids to go to their rooms. Show them who's boss so they'll never behave like that in front of you again.

This course would be an exertion of power and superiority by one side without any recognition of the other side's requirements. For the other side, this is at best "no-gain" and at worst is "loss" which falls into the negative upper-left quadrant "D." An embargo or a sanction is to stop any gain for the other side. In addition, to further exert one's will and power could range from minor loss to total annihilation.

Is winning always a good thing? In spiritual terms, our ultimate aspiration is to be the best we can be on all levels; we must strive to find the exceeding Self. From this perspective, the intention and desire to succeed and excel is admirable, and it is aligned with universal laws.

Human potential can be achieved through individual aspiration for self-mastery and growth at all levels. Throughout history, many societies and cultures have developed competitive activities, including sports or contests, to promote the pursuit of individual excellence. The Olympic Games are the perfect example of humanity coming together to compete and celebrate excellence, regardless of participants' race, color, culture, or nation. The ancient game of chess was developed to cultivate mental agility and strategic thinking. Wrestling and boxing are practiced to increase both mental alertness and physical strength. Contests like sailing or auto racing not only test the physical strength and mental stamina of competitors, but also the inventiveness and technical skills of participants. Even team sports, where the focus is not primarily on individual excellence, develop excellence in an individual's ability to work as part of a team driving toward a common goal.

But having a consummate winner also implies having a loser. Why do we choose a win-lose option, striving for our own gain while knowing it's intrinsically tied to another person's loss? It is, among other things, an instinctive urge to be in control, to display power and strength over others.

We rationalize it by saying:

- That's life.

- Someone has to be in charge.

- I deserve it.

- It's a jungle out there, and only the fittest survive.

It is our innate desire to do our best that propels us to grow, to be more creative and more constructive. As long as our intentions are aligned with this notion we are behaving at the edge of quadrant "A," which represents the absence of any gain for the other party. However, there is danger of falling into the negative quadrant "D" if the assertion of our will or power results in punishment, loss, or destruction of others. When we begin valuing our achievements only in terms of abasement of others, rivalry can become ugly. Certainly competition and rivalry have a place in a debate, a sporting tournament, or a chess match. But when we lose sight of our intention, mindless competition merely creates an antagonistic mindset and counterproductive outcomes—if not immediately, then over time.

Although playing to win is an acceptable and, indeed, expected behavior in the proper setting, during any negotiation, whether business or personal, a tone of aggression or dominance can be a barrier to reaching acceptable outcomes for all parties. Finding pleasure in the defeat of an opponent may be tolerable on some occasions, but striving for the annihilation of one's counterpart can defeat the object of negotiation by making the situation unbearable for the other party.

Since dominance is established and measured in inverse proportion to the success of the other party, there are two obvious ways of demonstrating superiority: one is through self-improvement, and the other through suppression of the other side's strengths. In the latter case, one's journey toward excellence is reduced to nothing more than wins-versus-losses score-keeping.

A Moment of Reflection on Why We Negotiate

Before continuing to the last quadrant of the diagram, let's take a moment to ask ourselves why we negotiate. It's astonishing to me how often people lack clarity on this fundamental question. You might also be surprised if you ask the question of a group of people and notice how many obscure or confused responses you receive.

After more than two decades of involvement in business, academia, marriage (!), and cross-cultural studies, I am content with my own answer. *We negotiate because we need something.*

Negotiation is a process of communication between two or more parties in the hope of enhancing their positions by satisfying their needs.

You come to the negotiating table because you *need* something. The other side also needs something, which is why *they're* at the table. Neither of you can satisfy your needs, at least not easily, without the help of the other party. This simple truism applies whether the negotiation is about complex issues in international relations or about a couple deciding where to go out to dinner.

In a later chapter discussing the Law of Strength, we'll have more to say on this topic. For now, keep in mind this fundamental principle: People negotiate because they need something.

That said, back to our exploration of the map of options and possible outcomes.

Option Four: Collaborative, Constructive, Integrative, Principled

Another possible response to Jasmine and David's—and my—"orange problem" is the option of sitting down and taking the time to investigate the underlying desires that precipitated the tug of war. What is the essence of each party's underlying need? In a simple case like this, we can just ask David and Jasmine why each of them needs the orange in the first place. Although the answer might seem obvious—they're hungry and they like oranges—it's often useful to get to the facts of the matter rather than relying on an assumption.

The same holds true in many other common negotiations: Why does your spouse need to go to *this* specific restaurant *tonight*? It might not be, as husbands tend to assume, yet another instance of a wife's characteristic obstinacy. She might have a two-for-one coupon for this restaurant that expires tomorrow!

Why does a customer need rush delivery? Can he be satisfied with rush delivery of a partial shipment, the balance to come later? Why is the seller of a house we're interested in buying insisting on a 30-day escrow closing?

Taking the time to understand the underlying need can often save time that would be wasted in irrelevant disputes over moot points.

On the spiritual level, any move (so long as it is conscious) begins with total awareness of the here and now. We can move forward and approach our goal only by first developing a clear appreciation of our strengths and attributes, as well as our desires and aspirations. Likewise, when we come into contact with others, staying in the here-and-now helps us avoid misleading presumptions and prejudices. There are pitfalls and dangers in entering a negotiation with faulty assumptions about the other's desires and aspirations. Misplaced assumptions invariably get us off on the wrong foot.

Therefore, I approached David and Jasmine with the essential question. Holding up the fruit that I've wrestled into my temporary protective custody, a kind of escrow account, I ask, "David, why do you need this orange?"

Clearly determined David tells me, "I'm thirsty, and orange juice would taste good right now."

I probe a little further: "Would anything else satisfy your desire for something wet and sweet? Maybe a bottle of water and a banana?"

Holding his ground, David says, "No!"

Next I moved down the path of discovery with Jasmine. "Jasmine, why do you need this orange?"

Jasmine reluctantly shares her secret. "Uncle Mehrad, I was trying to surprise my mom by baking her favorite orange peel cake for her birthday tonight!"

Now it becomes obvious that by giving the pulp and the juice to David and the rind to Jasmine, the needs of both will be met. Neither party in their side of our little three-cornered negotiation will have to settle for less than he or she desired, and none of the disputed resource will be wasted (David, eating the orange and throwing the skin away, or Jasmine using the skin and throwing the pulp away).

In the negotiation between both children and me, they stop fighting and I can finally get a nap. I benefit by moving directly toward my intended goal, the couch.

The problem can be solved on the tangible, physical level: Their needs are met, and I get some peace and quiet. On the intangible level as well, there will be emotional satisfaction, a sense of harmony, coming together, and peacefully sharing.

We shouldn't underestimate the value of less tangible gains as well as more quantifiable material gains:

- For my sister, coming home to a harmonious environment would probably be more precious to her than an orange-flavored birthday cake.

- The children have proven to me they're essentially thoughtful and well mannered, at least under the right conditions.

- And I've proven myself to be, in my eyes as well as in theirs, a responsible and caring adult who can deliver results, at least under the right conditions.

Those last two accomplishments are likely to bear considerably more fruit in the future than just one orange.

Not every challenge in negotiation can be resolved as neatly as our parable, naturally. But any potential path that moves us in a positive direction, at least partially, is worth exploring. It might provide a way station on our longer journey toward our goal.

A good outcome to a negotiation can always be plotted somewhere within the quadrant "A" of our diagram in which everyone benefits, at least to a degree. The ideal outcome is the maximum gain for all parties on or close to the collaboration point.

Why do we choose the option of collaboration?

- It has the potential to advance both parties toward their goals.

- It has the potential of discovering untapped resources so that no resources are wasted.

- It offers the best outcome energetically. It generates the potential for further collaboration and co-creation. Collaboration ignites synergetic power that can drive us forward in future relationships and have a positive effect on other negotiations.

- It makes life more meaningful and fulfilling.

- And, finally, although it takes time and effort up front to collaborate, the overall outcome can save a lot of wasted time, resources, and energy and be more efficient as a whole.

Option Five:
Compromise, Mutual Concession, Give and Take

One option suggested by students who have heard my story of Jasmine and David is frequently given with a matter-of-fact shrug: Cut the orange in half and give half to each of the kids. Certainly it could provide the most equitable solution to David and Jasmine's dilemma, but unless we explore all the options it could be a wasteful choice. Given what each child actually needed the orange for, had we jumped to this conclusion we would have wasted half of our resources. In this story, half an orange may not seem like a big loss, but in the grand scale of national and international transactions it could be what represents economic or political survival.

On the spiritual level, the concept of balance is powerful and meaningful. Buddha was enlightened by his discovery of what he called the Middle Way after many years of searching, and middle paths are promoted in many wisdom traditions. The essence of *yin* and *yang* in the Chinese tradition and *ha* and *tha* in Hinduism and yoga is about finding this middle point in any circumstance and being able to operate from there. Hence, when we arrive at the point at which we have to share a limited resource, compromise seems like the intelligent and spiritually guided approach.

It is only after we have explored all, and I mean *all*, possibilities, however, and have logically considered the assembled facts at hand, that we should come to this conclusion. It might indeed turn out to be the honorable and productive way, drawing from the positive essence of collaboration. But any shortcut leading to a premature conclusion in a rush to compromise is decidedly less than ideal and does not represent our highest aspirations, values, or spiritual nature.

Why would we choose a half-and-half option? We can choose it based on principled reasoning, or simply on the fact of limited resources. Or we might rationalize that it saves time or that there is no other viable option.

Arriving at a compromise through a collaborative process is without a doubt a win-win resolution. However, if we reach this conclusion because of insufficient creativity or a failure to remain open-minded, it can feel like a lose-lose situation, or at best an unsatisfying quasi-win for both sides.

The concepts of cooperation, collaboration, compassion, and "golden rules" of conduct are all part of our common psychological, social, and biological fabric. In a very literal sense, they're part of our nature. Many evolutionary processes went into building this into our genes. From a biological standpoint, the principle of kin selection is recognized to be part of human nature and the genes that promote compassion, sympathy, and love towards kin, those of the same family or clan serve the evolutionary purpose of ensuring that a set of genes are reproduced generation after generation.

The biological concept of Reciprocal Altruism offers a promising explanation for why humans behave compassionately. It speculates that compassion leads us to do good things for other people who then will return the favor; we see something of ourselves in a fellow human being, as if in a mirror, and instinctively feel that what benefits the other person benefits us.

This kind of compassion may be confined to a select group; a member of one clan might not see an advantage in aiding a member of another clan. The principle of reciprocal altruism might not strike us as proper altruism at all: There's something obviously self-serving about expecting to receive rewards for showing compassion or having a lack of compassion for those who are not of our own family, community, or tribe. Nevertheless, this impulse has given us an intuitive appreciation for altruism when we see it, and universally we accept the principle that a good deed is often, or at least it deserves to be, reciprocated by another good deed.

Option Six:
Mutual-Destruction, Lose-Lose

As I watched my niece and nephew tussle over the disputed orange, at one point every time Jasmine was close to grabbing it, David threatened to throw it out the window. A situation like this represents a low point in the win-lose quadrant "D." David gains nothing; his only enjoyment of the orange would be in savoring Jasmine's loss of the orange. *As long as I'm not getting what I want, I'll make sure you lose too,* "mutual destruction" which falls in lower-left quadrant "C."

The Possibilities of Interactions

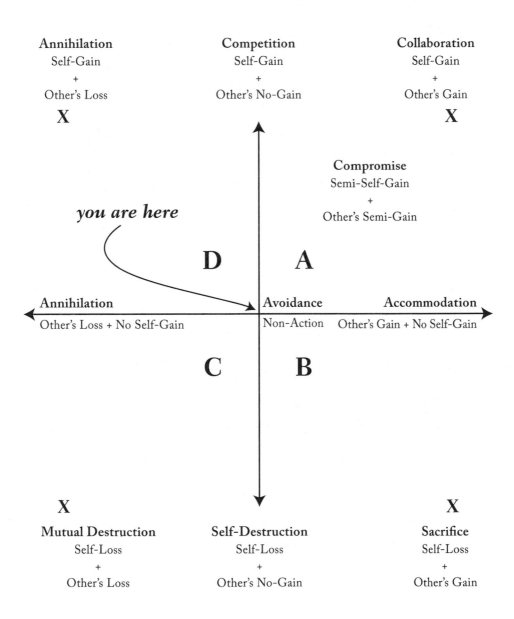

On a community or national level, lengthy strikes and walk-outs can fall into this category when unrealistic demands on each side threaten to drive each other to bankruptcy or starvation.

The NFL officials strike of 2012 that resulted in a three-month disruption of the season's games, is a good example. One Monday night contest between the Seattle Seahawks and the Green Bay Packers came close to putting the NFL out of business when the all-important trust in the authority of the officials who apply the rules of football broke down. Ill-qualified replacement officials hired by the league blew the biggest call of the game and unjustly awarded the Seahawks the winning touchdown as time expired, nearly touching off a riot in the stands. Now you can imagine the far-reaching negative ripple effect also caused headaches for players, coaches, the TV network, its advertisers, and countless football fans.

When I was watching David's and Jasmine's behavior moving toward mutual destructions the word "childish" would come to mind. Isn't it ironic that it happens frequently and at all levels? Here is an example of this in international negotiations in their book *Getting to Yes* by Roger Fisher and Bill Ury:

> In negotiations between the United States and Mexico, the U.S. wanted a low price for Mexican natural gas. Assuming that this was a negotiation over money, the U.S. Secretary of Energy refused to approve a price increase negotiated with the Mexicans by a U.S. oil consortium. Since the Mexicans had no other potential buyer at the time, he assumed they would then lower their asking price. But the Mexicans had a strong interest not only in getting a good price for their gas but also in being treated with respect and a sense of equality. The U.S. action seemed like one more attempt to bully Mexicans; it produced enormous anger. Rather than sell their gas, the Mexican government began to burn it off, and any chance of agreement on a lower price became politically impossible.[19]

This represents the opposite spectrum of collaboration: when the destruction of the other side is the goal even though its price is self-destruction.

DEFINING THE FIELD
FOR ESTABLISHING INTENTION

The map of our behavioral options for getting from where we are now to where we want to be lays out a landscape of divergent possibilities, winding paths, and many potential pitfalls. If how we choose to navigate through the map is not by conscious choice, we will be navigating on autopilot, out of unconscious, automatic, or reactionary motives. Clarifying our intentions means surveying the landscape and discovering the most promising path toward our objective, and allowing ourselves to be drawn forward by our spiritual urge to reach our highest potential, as well as driven by our individual aspirations. With that in mind, we can summarize what we've learned so far about enlightened negotiation.

SUMMARIZING THE LAW OF INTENTION

- Assess your current environment thoroughly.
- Assess the situation from a spiritual perspective.
- Analyze the cost and benefit of each option.
- Evaluate the risk of negative outcomes.
- Aim for collaboration and fulfilling each party's desires completely.
- Be open to compromise or "agreeing to disagree," but only after exhausting the potential of mutually beneficial collaboration.

3

The Law of Communication

The great enemy of communication, we find, is the illusion of it.[20]
—William H. Whyte

Communication is one of the central pillars of any negotiation or, indeed, any relationship between people. Bad communications lead to bad negotiations. A successful negotiation requires effective and clear communication.

In the second half of the 20th century, after radio was developed, we came to think of "communication" as synonymous with "broadcasting." We put our messages out "on the air," on the assumption someone would be at the receiving end, laboring at tuning-in a weak signal or tenuous connection.

With the advent of the Internet we've returned, in large part, to the earlier sense of communication as a one-to-one, back and forth exchange of information, although the participants can number in the billions.

In today's digital communication media, our messages are scrambled, broken down into bits, poured into a swirling system of interconnections only visualized as a "cloud," and then assembled and unscrambled at the receiving end. The system works only because at every step along the journey the integrity of the information is tested and verified.

We often use the words "hearing" and "listening" interchangeably, but strictly speaking they're distinct activities in the communication process. *Hearing* is a function of our physical sense array, the reception of sound. *Listening* is part of our cognitive array, processing raw data into comprehension, knowledge, and insight by decoding and interpreting the signals sent to us through our ears. Listening also means the conscious act of turning our ears toward sound we want to trace and choosing to give attention to the incoming signal.

Miscommunication between people arises not when we're hearing-impaired, but when we're *listening*-impaired, when a glitch or breakdown occurs at any stage along the process flowing from perception to comprehension.

Our tongues and ears somehow manage to take a mental concept in the mind of the speaker, scramble and dice it into a string of signals, transfer it across vast distances, and reconstitute the signals into more or less identical concepts in the mind of the listener. It can then be amplified with the catalyst of the receiver's own thoughts, feelings, and experiences. This complex process works miraculously well sometimes, especially when the listener verifies the integrity of the transmission through a feedback signal with the originator.

Communication requires a *sender*, a *message*, and a *receiver*. The effectiveness of communication is measured by the clarity of the message, its fidelity to what the sender intended after it has been conveyed.

THE SENDER

Communication, at the most basic human level, is the activity of sharing information, thoughts, emotions, or knowledge through an exchange system of speech, visual signals, manual writing, or behavior. This basic form—a direct, local, person-to-person communication—is the subject of most of this chapter.

Our technologies have vastly expanded our ability to signal each other with racing pulses of light and subatomic particles, and now we can spell out HELP! with coconuts on a beach and expect to have it noticed by orbiting satellites. Even so, the basics of face-to-face human communication have not been abandoned, only enhanced.

Communication is a multidimensional interaction, and the same intended message could be interpreted differently depending on countless factors, ranging from our physical condition (such as that of the renowned physicist Stephen Hawkings, who communicates by using a single cheek muscle attached to to a speech-generating device because of his paralysis from a motor-neuron disease) to the weather, the state of our political institutions and infrastructure, and even gamma rays and solar flares.

As a sender, you should keep in mind that much of what you're communicating—your true feelings, sentiments, and emotions—is conveyed by nonverbal signals. For those of us who are phone-oriented, we should realize that skill in controlling our tonality in phone conversations exponentially increases our odds of getting our message across. We should also be aware of *vocal interference,* the "signal noise" we introduce by using meaningless words such as *ah, um,* and *you know* that waste "bandwidth" and can be as distracting as a jackhammer in the background to sensitive listeners. People want clear and concise communications, especially from professionals.

THE MESSAGE

We must always ask ourselves: *How can we improve the message we want to communicate?* How can it be simpler or more comprehensive? How can it be framed to avoid premature rejection? What's the best way to deliver it? How can we be assured that is has been received and processed as we intended?

The whole point of communication is to transfer mental concepts from one person to another; therefore the message itself ought to be worth the effort. We should ask ourselves whether that's really true. What exactly are we communicating? Facts relevant to substantive issues? Educated opinions supported by trusted research? Rumors and gossip? Lies? Our own transitory emotional needs?

If we're bothering to connect with another person, the content of the message we intend to transmit should be meaningful and useful, sensitive and balanced, and courteous yet impactful enough to rate priority with the receiver.

THE RECEIVER

The receiver's comprehension of your message is the ultimate goal of your communication. As the architect of your communications, what can you do to enhance your receiver's receptivity? Would presenting the relevant facts in a different order not only convey the message more indelibly, but also convey the background context of your sentiments and emotions in a balanced way?

In the act of communicating, you constantly switch roles between sender and receiver. A good negotiator should take responsibility for coherent communication while wearing both hats.

How do you know if you're communicating clearly and comprehensively? The easiest way is simply to *ask* the listener to "ping" back to you what you've said, to test your signal strength and verify you're getting through.

When acting as receiver, seasoned negotiators want to make sure the signals they're receiving aren't distorted and that the message received is accurate according to what the other person intended to send. There's no shame in asking for confirmation or clarification. One way of validating the signals is to echo the messages back to the sender, rephrasing what was heard and evaluating the level of understanding at the receiving end. It's a useful habit to say from time to time, "If I understand you correctly, what you're saying is [X]. Is that correct?"

An enlightened negotiator not only takes an active role in transmitting validation signals back to the sender, but also stays attuned to the subliminal and emotional states of the sender. It's not only practical and wise in terms of fully equipping ourselves; sometimes it's simple human decency to ask, "When you were talking about implementing the new policy, I sensed some hesitation and unease. Caroline, is there more you want to tell me?"

Of course a face-to-face negotiation is preferable in most cases. However, there are times when we have no recourse except to use other formats, many of which might limit our personal ability to fully express all the nuances we detect in face-to-face interactions. Email, voice mail, and texting can be hindrances in this type of communication, yet there are also advantages in utilizing technology, such as ease of use, time saving, cost saving, and the ability to keep the momentum going. In addition, email offers us the ability to write, rewrite and fine-tune our message to perfection and, only when ready, send our message. The time we gain in using digital email compared to the "snail mail" of a generation ago can be profitably spent in honing our communications. But please take your time in order to take full advantage of this opportunity. Before you press the SEND key, just read what you wrote one more time. This saves a lot of hassles.

THE POWER OF THE SPOKEN WORD

In many wisdom traditions, sound is the source of creation. "In the beginning was the word," the Bible says, setting Creation in motion with a mighty voice. The passage rings true to our experience as mere humans: We manifest our intentions in the material world through what we say.

Some years ago, I attended a symposium in India on the philosophy and spiritual practices of the Zoroastrianism, a religion dating to six thousand years before the birth of Jesus that significantly influenced Christianity and Judaism. I had the good fortune to travel with a group of Parsis, one of the few remaining Zoroastrian groups, which had migrated to India from ancient Iran to avoid persecution by Muslim invaders. The Parsis are known for their lifestyle and philosophy emphasizing righteousness. My fellow travelers shared with me that Parsis are extremely conscious of the power of words, and their social practices involve honoring a person's spoken words at all times in the certainty that everything we say will be made manifest in

reality. They recognize a cosmic principle that empowers the actualization of spoken words.

Parsis show the utmost diligence in their speech and only ver-
balize that which expresses truth. For example, if a Parsi says, "I will
meet you at 10 a.m." he makes sure to show up at 10 a.m. When
he says, "I'll pay you back the money in one week," you can bank
on his honoring his word. These acts of absolute certainty in the truth
of the spoken word that a person will follow through on one's commitment to do something, express in action their spiritual belief in
a universal law of creation and forms the foundation of their social
order. For a Parsi, saying anything that isn't true, or won't be true, is
simply unthinkable. Among their neighbors, they have a centuries-
old reputation for integrity, honesty, trustworthiness, and reliability.
(It's often said that in the colonial era in India when British authori-
ties were setting up the banking system, they would hire only Parsis
as bank tellers.)

The members of this community live in a network of trusted relationships. They support and are supported by an environment of trust
that enables them to act within their community without reserva-
tion or hesitation, eliminating the need for institutions to guard their
interests and ensure restitution in case of default. Those outside the
community also feel totally secure in their transactions with the Parsis and usually forego the protections normally included in agreements
with non-Parsis.

Yoga teaches us that our energy or universal life force flows throughout the body in channels called *nadis*, somewhat corresponding to the
chi lines in T'ai Chi practice and the *meridians* in Chinese medicine.
The most esoteric practice of yoga details 72,000 *nadis*.

In Yoga, it is believed these channels intersect at various hubs or
chakras, a term meaning *wheels* in Sanskrit, that are located throughout the body, with seven of these energy centers located along the

spine. We might visualize them as channels of flowing light radiating from a central hub like the spokes of a turning wheel.

Each chakra governs certain aspects of our behavior and life functions, such as survival, creativity, self-worth, love, communication, intuition, and self-actualization. (In a chapter to come, I'll discuss Abraham Maslow's Hierarchy of Needs, another way of visualizing the relationships among various essential aspects of our being.)

The energy center that relates to communication is located in the throat area, naturally enough, and is called the *Vishuda* chakra. Yoga adherents think of this chakra as not only our instrument of communication, but how we manifest in the material world generally. How we use this energy source has a significant impact on the dynamic progress we make in our personal, business, and spiritual lives.

Extra credit:

What is the most powerful word in your language?

Your name! When we hear our names we feel a strong and deep connection. When our name is used properly, it represents acknowledgement, respect, and connection. Personalize your communications and use people's name rather than their roles or titles.

Tonality

Raise your words, not your voice. It is rain that
grows flowers, not thunder.[21]—Rumi

Whenever we speak, tonality plays a large part in our effectiveness as communicators. In every verbal communication, there are nuances of meaning carried in our tone of voice. The intention of your message (to welcome, dominate, threaten, or reassure), and your own state of mind (enthusiastic, timid, hostile, or inviting) will come through your tonality regardless of the words you choose. And yet many of us assume we have no control over the voice we're born with and never bother to evaluate or try to improve our tonality.

To build control over your tonality, the first step is to listen to your own voice. Use your smartphone to record yourself and then listen to the audio clip closely several times. One exercise is to repeat a simple sentence "How are you?" and vary your inflection by putting the emphasis on a different word each time. Also try to say the sentence with no word emphasized, meaning a flat intonation.

You'll notice that with the emphasis on the first word, it's as if we're reaching out, perhaps to build rapport or seek acceptance. Shifting the emphasis alters the meaning slightly, perhaps from *What's the matter?* (the "New York greeting") to *Forget about everyone else, I want to know about you.* The flat-tonality version might sound robotic, but a neutral tone can also indicate distance and formality, perhaps acknowledging the equal footing of parties in a conversation.

When we hear ourselves in recordings, many of us dislike our own voices (the acoustics of our skulls means we normally hear our voices as no one else does), but it's worth getting comfortable with one's voice. As an enlightened negotiator, there's value in expanding your ability to communicate with nuance and in knowing how you're being perceived.

Here's a Simple Exercise:

Record yourself saying "Where did you get this information?"

First say it as if you are a military commander. Then say it as if you were speaking to a child, either with doubt in your voice or with awe and appreciation. Try saying it as if you were talking to a close friend, and then as a lawyer questioning a witness.

For each different situation you can visualize saying this in a slightly different voice or perhaps in a very different voice, and the amazing thing is that we already have these many voices inside us.

Open-ended versus Closed-ended Questions

In *Hamlet*, Shakespeare has Polonius encounter Hamlet reading a book. When Polonius asks the moody young prince what he's reading,

Hamlet replies with a conversation deflating one-word answer: "Words." (Parents of teenagers will recognize this tactic.)

Ah, but if you know your Shakespeare, you'll remember that's not entirely accurate. Hamlet actually repeated the one-word answer *three times, saying,* "Words, words, words"—a statement that speaks volumes about Hamlet's despairing search for meaning and direction.

As enlightened negotiators, whenever you ask a question you should be aware that not all questions fall into the same category. Some open the floodgates to information exchange, while others close down the flow, perhaps to a dead stop. Questions are a useful tool in our communications, and we should know which direction to turn the wrench.

What we call "closed-ended questions" are ones that require shorter answers than what we term "open-ended questions." Open-ended questions are easy to identify because they require or invite more than a one-word reply. They're the essay rather than the multiple-choice prompt of everyday life. They're useful to solicit any facts available and learn more about a counterpart's feelings and motives. But we should be prepared to receive and process the flow, not let it go to waste. When you're engaged and attentive to the extended answer you've asked for, you establish rapport with your counterpart.

The following are some examples of closed-ended questions and open-ended questions.

Closed-ended Questions

(These can often be answered in one word.)

Can I help you?

Have you been with the company long?

Do you want to handle it this way?

Is this what you want to achieve?

Does this timetable work for you?

Do you have more information?

Open-ended Questions

(These questions require an explanation)

> How can I help you?
>
> How long have you been with the company?
>
> How do you want to handle this?
>
> What are your concerns?
>
> What are the objectives you're trying to satisfy?
>
> Tell me more about this piece.

You'll notice that closed-ended questions aren't necessarily just answered by a yes or no. They can also be given to expect either/or answers, or set up to offer limited choices, sometimes with (as computer programmers call it) a built-in "default" choice. At that point, they become *pointed* or *leading* questions, useful for driving a negotiation briskly forward, finalizing specific terms, or concluding the transaction gracefully:

- Which is better for you: Tuesday or Wednesday?
- Are you paying cash or using a credit card?
- Will there be anything else?

THE ART OF LISTENING

Active listening is an important way to bring about
changes in people.[22]—Carl Rogers

Hearing is one of the five cognitive senses we're born with, but *listening* is an art and an acquired skill. Most of us have never been trained how to listen. When we listen poorly or not at all, we have gaps or breakdowns in communication. Sometimes even a subtle miscommunication can have costly results, such as a lost sale, an angry confrontation, a broken heart, or a broken home—all because someone wasn't listening attentively.

Although listening constitutes much of the time we spend in communicating with others, it's typically the least developed of our communication skills. *Forbes* magazine reported[23] that in a typical business day, we spend 45 percent of our time listening, 30 percent of our time talking, 16 percent reading, and nine percent writing. Eighty-five percent of what we know we've learned through listening, but the average person listens with a 25 percent rate of comprehension. And yet fewer than two percent of all professionals have had formal training in techniques for improving their listening and understanding skills

In perhaps one of the most significant efforts toward understanding and promoting the importance of listening in the twentieth century, in 1979 Sperry Corporation (one of the early mainframe manufacturers and a company that later became Unisys) embarked on an ambitious experiment. As part of a public relations campaign, rather than focusing on a new product or service, Sperry's marketing team put the emphasis of the campaign on people and the power of communication, with the core of the messaging centered on *listening*. Sperry Corporation's slogan became "We understand the importance of listening."

Tests[24] made as part of the study disclosed that immediately after listening to a 10 minute oral presentation, the average consumer or employee has heard, understood, properly evaluated and retained only half of what was said. Within 48 hours, that sinks another 50 percent. The final level of effectiveness comprehension and retention is only 25 percent! Even worse, as ideas are communicated from one person to the next, they can become distorted by 80 percent.

If the company were to live up to its slogan, it was apparent that listening, including comprehension and retention, would first have to be cultivated within the company. To establish a new culture of listening in the Sperry workplace and among its managers, over the next five years, 44,000 employees were educated in the art and science of listening, and Sperry set forth on a quest to spread awareness of the importance of listening, not just within the company, but with its customers, suppliers, and shareholders.

The Four Elements of Listening

The most basic of all human needs is the need to understand and be understood. The best way to understand people is to listen to them.[25]—Ralph Nichols,
the founder of the International Listening Association

There are four elements of good listening: focusing, hearing, understanding, and remembering.

Focusing

First you have to establish the intention of consciously listening and create an awareness of the importance of listening. This by itself creates a more open and receptive mind that can focus on both the verbal and nonverbal (e.g., body language) aspects of communication. How often do we see conflict growing out of a situation where one side complains that the other doesn't listen!

Everyone we speak to deserves to be heard in turn, whether she's our neighbor, our employer or employee, parent or child, physician or patient. Everyone expects to have a chance to express themselves once they've listened to you, so prepare to give them what they expect.

Many barriers to focusing arise simply from the distraction of our internal dialogue when we're trying to multitask too much. Sometimes we're caught daydreaming. Sometimes we jump to conclusions, disrespectfully fast-forwarding over what we assume the other person is likely to say. Sometimes we're just bored or tired, and our focus drifts to the style of delivery rather than content of what the other person is saying.

Training in practices such as yoga and meditation can help you increase your attention spans and patience, and help you to stay aware and mindful while maintaining an inward harmonious tranquility. Like any other kind of discipline, learning to control your focus requires guidance and regular practice.

But it's easy to begin with a simple exercise, drawn from the ancient practice of concentration known as Dharana, as a step toward the level of mindfulness achieved through meditation. Take a bell or chime to a more or less silent location. Ring it, and listen until the sound fades away completely. Concentrate on noticing when that happens. You'd be surprised how difficult this can be. Often the voice of our thoughts intervenes, or some dust speck in the environment captures our attention while the sound is still resonating, and we miss hearing the tail end (or at least fail to have a clear memory of hearing it). But after a few tries, you should get the hang of just listening, patiently, to nothing but the ringing sound to its very end.

Now take the bell to an environment with quiet background noises like bird chirps or the rustling of leaves in the wind, and again try listening to the sound of the bell until the ringing fades away, while filtering-out the background "noise."

When you feel you've mastered listening with all of your awareness to the sound of the bell, despite distractions, try listening mindfully to one of the background sounds while filtering out the sound of the bell. Once you've accomplished this third step, you'll have practice not only in focusing, but also in *shifting* your focus.

Hearing

You can't expect to hear, let alone listen attentively to, what someone is saying if your cell phone keeps chirping, vibrating, meowing, or playing "Help Me, Rhonda" by the Beach Boys to signal that someone else wants your attention. Some people claim they can offer their undivided attention while alarm bells are going off in the background, but as for me, I can't really concentrate on a conversation over the phone in an airport waiting area with the public address system blaring away, or at a conference in a hotel ballroom with hundreds of people talking at once. We certainly need to train our minds and ears to focus and ignore distractions, but that doesn't mean we shouldn't try to minimize those distractions we have control over. If the situation makes it difficult to have a conversation, it's usually possible to say, "Can we set up a time to discuss this?"

Understanding

When someone is explaining something to you, it's not enough to listen passively, expecting the other person to do all the work of getting across the information. You must also put effort into reaching out to grasp the message you're receiving. You should do all you can, both intellectually and emotionally, to associate the other person's points with your own frame of reference, perhaps by mentally recasting the speaker's message in words of your own, thinking of analogies from your own experience, or connecting new concepts with similar ideas you've thought about in the past. As negotiators, you should keep in mind that the whole point of listening is not merely to *look* receptive but also to *be* receptive and to incorporate into your own sphere of knowledge whatever you take in.

As we listen, there may be things going on inside us, but often we assume it's our turn to remain silent and restrain our signals. In fact, we can (and usually do, without realizing it) actively participate in drawing forth the speaker by acknowledging points we grasp and agree with, empathizing aloud, and even paraphrasing back to the speaker what she is saying. *Active* listening ought to include giving such feedback (in moderation, without interrupting or judging or "taking the floor") so the other party can monitor our level of engagement and interest, and so we can bring potential misunderstandings to light immediately, before they can lead us too far astray.

Remembering

If communication is to have purpose, the information you've received ought be available to you later when it might be of most value. You

someone to like us, espe-
in which to do so?

ting our movements and
unterpart, neither getting

0 words per minute tends
lay, in the age of rapid-fire
ixties, on the other hand,
per minute) feels uncom-
same rate might even feel
certainly want to be your-
t your speaking rate to fit
f take-up while still being
t of the time in daily life,

our communication style,
ce length, and body lan-
the other person, without

an once said, *adjust your*
(or prudent deliberation)
terpart and then gradually
stablished congruence with
you—they're likely to fol-
ed negotiation the goal is
sly, like soldiers marching
ast age swinging perfectly
spike to the rhythm of a

need a way to capture the communication accurately and then mentally label it and file it away among your other experiences, someplace where you can retrieve it easily. How we choose to categorize it in our mental filing system—perhaps in the "another boring meeting" cabinet? Or maybe in the "trouble brewing" inbox—can make considerable difference.

Spoken conversation has the disadvantage, compared to email and texting, of not normally being recorded word for word. It persists only in our memories, in fragments stored in several people's minds, as experienced from separate points of view, a situation that invites conflicting versions down the road.

Taking down written notes can be helpful, if it's convenient and appropriate. (Some conversations involve a pledge of confidentiality, which note taking might be seen as violating.) Even without written notes, we can enhance the clarity, accuracy, and vividness of our memory if we make an effort to package the words of a conversation together with as much "situational awareness" of the moment as we can sweep in: "We were waiting in the lobby because it had started to rain, and you were wearing a blue windbreaker. We had just been talking about the need for a prototype budget when you brought up the possibility of crowdfunding. . . ." can be almost as good as a time-stamp on a signed document for establishing the authenticity of a disputed recollection.

FRAMING YOUR MESSAGE

When it comes to delivering a message, perhaps one of the most effective and least used skills is framing that message, meaning to plan precisely how we will present our case to others. Framing structures a conversation along specific lines, viewed in a certain light or from a specific perspective.

For instance:

Two young men from a rough part of the city joined a monastery, hoping to free themselves of the burdens of the street life they'd

known. Among the burdens they brought with them
habit, and by the afternoon prayers on their first day,
perate for a cigarette.

One of them couldn't stand it any longer, so he
head priest's office and asked, "Say Father, is it okay if v
we pray?"

He walked back to his friend with bad news. No d

"Let me take a shot at this," the other said. He
priest's door, waited meekly to be admitted, and th
with a show of humility and reverence.

"Father, are we permitted to pray while we smoke:
"Of course!" said the priest told him. "Go right ah
See? It's all in the way the question is framed.

Framing is a familiar method politicians use. Terr
relief" and "no child left behind" tend to be better rece
ting your government services" and "giving your kids lo
ized tests."

Even the scientific community chooses its lang
awareness of the associations certain words trigger. Th
for the worldwide climate effects caused by human act
on, *global warming*. The term fell out of favor, however,
it's misleading (the effects aren't limited to warming), b
the words themselves sounded like a drumbeat of do
generated resistance to the scientists' message. *Climate*
preferred term, is intentionally neutral and open-end
explanation of "What kind of change?" and framing th
call for objectivity and reason rather than shrill alarm.

Restaurants use framing to entice customers and s
atmosphere. In a restaurant chain's marketing study w
was offered "chocolate cake" while another was off
dish identified as "Belgian Black Forest Double-Ch
increased the sale by 27 percent and improved attitud
food and towards the restaurant (Cornell University

agree with that person. So how do we get
cially if we only have a short period of time

One technique involves *pacing*—adju
communications so we're in step with our c
too far ahead nor falling behind.

A relatively slow speaking rate of 80-1
to be boring to a young, energetic person to
information. To a person in their fifties or
a faster conversational pace (140-160 word
fortably hurried. To an elderly person, the
disorienting or threatening. Although you
selves when you speak, it's possible to adju
the situation or match your listener's rate
true to your natural voice. We do this mo
almost unconsciously.

It's also possible to intentionally pace
including our cadence, breathing, senten
guage, to be "on the same frequency with
falling into mimicking him.

To change another's behavior, a wise
own. Set an example of brisk productivit
by first synchronizing yourself to your cou
increasing or retarding the pace. If you've
the other person—if they see themselves i
low your lead. Remember that in enlighte
for all parties to move forward harmonio
in cadence or the railroad workers of a
syncopated hammer blows upon the sam
inspiring spiritual.

THE RITUALS OF COMMUNICATION

Because we seek communication, not confrontation, we should also be conscious of the symbolism of where we physically place ourselves in relationship with our counterparts. Simply by squaring off on opposite sides of a table, like football teams across the line of scrimmage, a message is sent that we must think of each other as adversaries. Then confrontation is all but guaranteed.

The notion of using seating arrangements to spur consensus-building has endured throughout history, from kiva circle gatherings of Native Americans to the famous round table of the Paris peace talks at the end of the Vietnam War. The horseshoe shape of the United Nations Security Council was also designed to signal equality and mutual respect, and to defuse, to some extent at least, confrontational mindsets. The circle in effect puts us all on the same side, without the hierarchy implicit in sitting "higher" or "lower" or at the "head" or "foot" of a conference table, and allows the parties to look at the challenges and obstacles before them from a shared perspective. As a result, we can use our communication skills to advance our views and goals as aggressively as necessary without pushing them "at" our counterpart. The true adversary, after all, is the problem we're going to solve together and the needs that must be addressed—not each other.

If you find yourself sitting across from your counterpart in a negotiation situation, consider breaking the symmetry by turning your body to a slight angle or moving to the other person's side while you go over documents. When you change the physical configuration, you also alter the dynamics of the interaction on a biological level since our bodies already know how difficult it is to have a fist-fight with someone who's sitting next to us. By altering something as basic as an uncomfortable eyeball-to-eyeball seating arrangement, we disrupt fixed assumptions and begin to move from confrontation to *co*-frontation.

SILENCE: THE GOLDEN TOOL

Silence is not sleep. Silence is alert. Silence speaks. Silence creates.
Silence silences.[27]—Swami Veda Bharati

As much as we have discussed the nature of effective communication, it's useful to appreciate the power and value of silence, if used properly. In any sales pitch or persuasive argument, the most powerful move after the message has been delivered is to wait in silence for the other person to make the next move. As any experienced salesperson knows, continuing to talk once the point has been made only leads to diminishing returns.

It's not enough to use silence only at the conclusion of presenting one's case. It's also important to pause and invite feedback at regular intervals during the negotiation. We're all conditioned to keep the conversational ball rolling, but rather than giving in to the impulse to keep talking just to fill an awkward silence or to press ahead to summarize what we've said, we should practice coming to a full stop and pausing. Allow the other person to be drawn in to fill the empty space. Trust stillness, and see what emerges. You might be very pleasantly surprised.

A wonderful story was told to me by Peter Davis, co-founder of the IDEA health and fitness association (the largest such organization in the world, with over 65,000 members/subscribers internationally).[28]

Peter was in the midst of a three-cornered negotiation. One was a major TV network and the other one was the largest international health food company. One of the final rounds of discussion was a conference call with the network executives and their attorneys in New York, the food company executives and their attorneys in Chicago and the IDEA's attorney in Los Angeles, and Peter in San Diego. Peter recalls that after a cordial opening statement and introduction of the parties, one network attorney immediately embarked on a nonstop, aggressive polemic without giving Peter any opening to speak.

Suddenly a dial tone made Peter aware that he'd been accidentally cut off from the conference call. He quickly attempted to reconnect with his attorney in Los Angeles to let him know of the technical difficulty, but the line was busy.

"After more than half an hour of waiting," Peter told me, "my phone rang. It was my attorney, bubbling over with delight. He couldn't stop praising me for my masterful performance during the conference call. Astonished and totally in the dark, I asked him which part of my masterful performance he was referring to.

"He said, '*You* know—that moment when the network attorney had presented a totally revised version of the contract and he asked you what you thought about it. And there was *dead silence*. Beautiful! I could hear him sweating over the phone. The next thing I knew, he'd folded his hand and was back to talking about the original terms. He was a pussycat from that point on. That silence must have scared the pants off him. I've never heard anything so powerful."

"Naturally," Peter told me, "I didn't bother to tell him about the technical glitch."

In the Sanskrit language there is a word, *svaatantrya*, that means "free will coming from the voice of one's true self." There is no exact English equivalent of the concept represented by the Sanskrit word, but the closest thing might be "non-reactivity." Think about the sense of empowerment and independence you would feel if your actions and thoughts *didn't* arise as reactions to situations and to others' actions, but simply flowed forth as expressions of your essential nature and priorities. Instead of being merely reactive, your words (and silences) would be authentically *responsive*.

Being non-reactive is, admittedly, a true challenge—not just on an emotional level, but also on a physiological one. Our brains are wired to be thoughtlessly reactive, as a survival mechanism.

A self-observant person will notice that, in a long discussion, quite often we begin to mimic the voice, tone, facial expressions, gestures, and positional body language of the person we're speaking to. They frown, we frown; they raise their voice, we raise ours. This is due to what neuroscientists have termed *mirror neurons,* our brain cells that fire with equal energy whether we perform an action or perceive someone else performing it. Mirror neurons help us learn by watching, and help us understand others' emotions, motives, and intentions through the direct experience of our own bodies.

But the phenomenon can also lead to emotional contagion, when we can "catch" a bad mood from someone else. Our co-worker scowls, triggering the same muscles in our own face. Scowling makes us feel bad, and the co-worker can see from our expression that we're upset, so they feel bad for us in turn. In an instant, we're both caught in a negative feedback loop. Of course, it's just as easy to "catch" a good mood, too. But even so, do we really want our emotions to be at the mercy of others' moods?

Practicing silence will help you begin to be "centered" in stillness, a position of strength in which you can feel your own emotions and act from your own volition, not on the reflex of mirror neurons. We have to feel comfortable with silence in order to be non-reactive, and most of us never learn to use the power of silence effectively because we never achieve that level of comfort with not having conversation. For many of us, sitting alone in a quiet room is almost intolerable for more than a few minutes. Practicing periods of silence as part of your daily life by setting aside time to turn off the phone, the radio, and television to just sit in stillness and tranquility, will begin to introduce you to its powerful potential. Once you're on a friendly basis with silence, you'll begin to recognize how vulnerable we all are to the emotional states of others, how much of our lives we spend being bounced about by the voices and tensions around us, and in aping other people. Eventually you'll be able to reach into your inner reserve and listen to the guidance of your own heart.

There's a technique for breaking negative emotional feedback loops that's relatively simple: The moment you observe a furrow of anxiety developing on the brow of a person you're interacting with, "deploy countermeasures" by reaching inward toward your center, that source of tranquility and confidence. Your thoughts will be reflected in your own face, your tone of voice, gestures, and body language. Then watch as the other person's mirror neurons take over and the shadows disappear from her face.

HAVE A BIAS TOWARD "YES"

Some of you may worry that adopting methods of sensitive communication means you will not be able to make your ideas understood. But it is always much easier to communicate what you need to communicate if you avoid negativity.

At the ashram of Swami Veda Bharati, an internationally renowned Vedic scholar, there are signs around the grounds that read, "Please let the flowers bloom." Swami Veda is quick to point out that there are no signs saying "Do not pick the flowers." The meaning of the two messages is essentially the same, but the first is phrased positively while the second is a warning suggesting punishment for a transgression. Communication can be considered successful when:

1. You have made your position, perception, and intention understood.

2. You have shown the other party respect, preserved their honor, and understood their position, perception, and intention.

As you have seen throughout this chapter, successful communication in the service of negotiation requires a high degree of self-awareness and the willingness to cultivate some important skills. But perhaps the most important lesson of all is this: In any negotiation, you must take full responsibility for furthering your own point of view in a way in which the other party can hear it. There is no point in casting blame on "unreasonable" or "close-minded" listeners. As it says in The Bhagavad-Gita, "It is but the speaker's flaw that the listener has not understood his intent."

SUMMARIZING THE LAW
OF COMMUNICATION

- Make sure you hear, and furthermore make sure you listen.

- Make sure your message is clear.

- Deliver a congruent message with your body language and tonality.

- As an Enlightened Negotiator, take the responsibility to make sure that you said was what was heard.

- Use open-ended questions for information gathering and clarification.

- Use closed-ended questions for conclusion and finalizing your agreement.

4

The Law of Strength

Knowledge itself is power.[29]—Francis Bacon, *Meditationes Sacrae*

Pamela, a smart and determined professional in her field, came to me for help in negotiating a crucial opportunity for advancement of her career, but the eventual outcome of Pamela's situation also proved enlightening for her in a broader, more personal sense. Her story is a useful illustration of the concept of *strength* in enlightened negotiation. Why is strength essential? What forms can it take? Where do we look to find the source of our own strength?

By every outward appearance, Pamela was an intelligent, energetic, driven, and positive young woman with a bright future in corporate marketing. When she came to me, she had been working for three years for one of the largest accounting firms in the United States. She had been hired to jump-start marketing efforts in their Western Region. Within the first year, her vision for what needed to be done, supported by her dedication and enthusiasm, had generated a surge of new business for her firm as her plans were implemented.

Two years later Pamela was promoted to a management role in her department. Although it came with a welcomed pay increase, the position entailed extra responsibilities and a willingness to take on additional, lateral workloads. Not long after her promotion, Pamela's immediate supervisor was faced with a health challenge that often required him to be absent from the office. Pamela pitched in to help and eventually took over many of his responsibilities, assuming it would be only for a brief period of time while he recovered. Then the firm set about expanding into a new area, an undertaking with a plan for hiring new employees, although so far not a single new staff member had been added to her department.

By any measure, the load on Pamela's plate was way too heavy. Yet, with her cheerful manner and her teamwork-promoting attitude, Pamela had kept up morale in the department despite the hard work and long hours. But this was at a significant cost to her personal life. By the time she came to me, Pamela had been trying to communicate her concerns to her superiors for six months, asking for more balanced responsibilities and suitable pay, but to no avail.

Two months before we met, Pamela had been informed that her original supervisor's health had deteriorated; he would not be coming back to work. Due to a corporate restructuring, she would be reporting to a new supervisor, a recent hire based in New York who had no direct experience with her department.

Despite her misgivings, Pamela found her new boss to be both professional and friendly. They'd had two phone conversations in which she discussed her position, that she deserved promotion and additional staff in light of her expanded responsibilities and her excellent performance during a difficult period. Her boss was sympathetic but evasive. Pamela shared with me some of the emails she had written to him. Although her boss had responded to all of them, her specific requests were either regretfully denied or simply dismissed.

Naturally, Pamela was frustrated. Clearly she was involved in a crucial negotiation affecting the path of her career, if not her whole life, but it was going nowhere; she had no way even to bring her boss to the bargaining table. She felt powerless and confused. Was she being treated this way because she's a woman, or because she stood out as being younger than most of the management team? Or was it something else, some weakness in her character that made her unfit for leadership? How could she fight back?

Pamela and I met a few days before her boss was scheduled to visit the West Coast office, the first time she would be meeting him face-to-face. If she were to confront him and press her case, it would be now or never.

I asked her, "What is it that you're asking from him?"

She said, "With all the responsibilities I have and what I've accomplished during this tough period, I deserve to be a director."

"So Pam, if your boss said, 'You're a director,' you will be happy for the next few years. Correct?"

There was a hesitation in her "I guess so."

"Pam, let me put it another way," I said. "What could your new boss offer you that *would* make you happy?"

"Well, social media marketing is my forte, and I know exactly what needs to be done . . ." Again, there was a pause in her voice, a falling-off of energy, and I sensed we needed to get the root of it.

"Let's forget about your boss and the directorship and social media marketing," I said. "Let me ask you this: Picture yourself meeting in a few days, not with your boss, but with a fairy godmother who can wave a magic wand and grant you the career of your dreams. What would you ask for?"

"I've been asking myself the same question, though I don't admit it," Pam laughed. "Maybe accounting just isn't for me anymore. I mean, my colleagues are wonderful people and the challenges are exciting. But, you know, my background was in the fashion industry. I never pictured myself working at an accounting firm. It just sort of happened."

I recognized a situation common to all too many Pamelas in the corporate world. Here we have someone who is drawn to take on challenges and to excel, to scale the rocky peaks of corporate management. For a Pamela, it's often satisfying on a purely personal level to recognize the value of her achievements, even if others don't, and to imagine that career advancement naturally follows. The soul of an artist inside a Pamela, however—the longing for creativity and stimulation, achievement of a personal vision, recognition from kindred souls—seldom finds fulfillment in cubicles and corridors, among charts of regional revenues.

Once she had familiarized herself (with characteristic energy) with the standard techniques, Pamela proved to be a good negotiator in the meeting with her boss. She effectively documented her case in terms an accountant would understand and demonstrated her value to the firm and the potential contribution to its success (as well as her boss's) that she could make if she were given proper resources and authority. She received her promotion and the title of Director.

After some months, I heard from Pamela and was eager to hear how she was doing in her new position.

"I've asked for a demotion, for my old position back," she told me. "I've been miserable in my new job. The good news is that I've enrolled in courses in fashion and design, and that's making me happy."

Pamela was able to climb the ladder with her determination and negotiation techniques (she was a good *negotiator*), BUT the ladder was against the wrong wall! (She was not an *enlightened negotiator*.)

Rather than feeling powerless, Pamela had begun to find her position of strength, the start of a long process of discovery. She discovered information of real value: her true needs and desires.

THE SOURCE OF OUR STRENGTH

In order to negotiate, you need the strength to hold firm to your own interests and the leverage to move the other side toward an outcome that benefits you as well as them. In a wrestling match, physical strength is central to the contest, yet *mental* strength is the ultimate key to seizing the moment when an opponent's footing is unsure or his center of gravity off-balance, the point when he can be tipped to one's advantage.

Once your intention is clearly conceived, you then need power to move forward and strength to endure the long path to your goal. An enlightened negotiator recognizes that true strength and power have intangible forms that vastly outweigh mere material displays of power. Lofty skyscrapers or bank accounts, legions of lawyers, fleets of limos or bulldozers or armored tanks all shrink in comparison to the limitless power of the mind and spirit, the life force within us all, as history has proven often enough.

An enlightened negotiator finds mental strength, above all, in truth: accurate information, refined knowledge, and their application in the process we call wisdom.

Let's revisit a question we posed in chapter 2: Why do we negotiate?

We negotiate because we need something. Negotiation is a process of communication between two or more parties hoping to satisfy their separate needs. Satisfaction of our needs is the goal compelling our negotiation.

If you don't need anything, you can walk through the marketplace deaf to, or simply amused by the abstraction of, the calls of vendors and pitches of advertisers. They may need your money to put food on their own tables, but your belly is full. It's only when you're aware of your own hunger, your own lack of something, that the bargaining can begin.

This is a universal fact: All parties involved in a negotiation are there for their own needs. A party's motivation might be greedy self-interest or enlightened self-interest, for the enrichment of one or the benefit of many; in either case *self*-interest is involved. Therefore, when we speak of the strength of knowledge, the most valuable is knowledge about one's self and about the other party's sense of self. Together, this knowledge delineates the context in which we negotiate.

Second, as you draw on the power of knowledge by exploring the needs of each party, it's of utmost importance to make sure the needs you discover at the root of your motivation are aligned with your authentic selves, values, and belief systems, that they are worthy of the evolved consciousness of humanity as a whole—that they aren't just whim or impulse, the superficial, or the distorted mirage of a more distant, truer need. We must extract the innate, upwardly striving desires of our nature to counterbalance desires that form in our minds and hearts at their weakest moments. We will be launching our power toward our goal from this platform of information; it is essential that we are positioned solidly on the *right* platform.

To fully evaluate what you know, you must tap into another source of your mental strength: wisdom.

Wisdom and Knowledge

Where is the wisdom we have lost in knowledge? Where is the knowledge we have lost in information?[30]—T. S. Eliot, *The Rock*

It has been said that there's never before been a time when so many people know so little about so much.

Perhaps you've also heard it said that knowledge is information, while wisdom is experience.

Knowledge is having useful information—facts and data true to reality—available when you need it, while wisdom is the ability to consciously *apply* knowledge in making good decisions. In a sense, knowledge is a tool and wisdom is the craft that makes use of that tool.

Knowledge is stored in your memories, while wisdom is a part of your consciousness. Wisdom is knowledge in action, being used effectively in the context of the moment but with a view toward the future. Once we've responded to a situation with true wisdom, we become cognizant of its rippling effect across time and the web of relationships connecting all of us.

Wisdom is making use of knowledge within a greater context and with a broader vision, for far-reaching effects.

THE SOURCE OF OUR MOTIVATIONS

The life force within us drives us in one direction or another based on physical, psychological, and social aspects of our beings. Whether we're buying a house or car, planning a family vacation, or applying for a new job, our situation has been shaped by specific needs that are the source of our motivations. They're what's brought us to the product-comparison web page, the market, the bargaining table. On a different scale, the needs at the root of corporate policies, departmental expenditures, and boardroom decisions that might include the need for expansion or contraction of the company, development of a less costly product or a more effective slogan—are what brings the company to the negotiating table. The same applies to diplomats in international negotiations, or community activists, or volunteers with charitable organizations, where "underlying self-interest" and "satisfaction of needs" might seem like odd ways of describing the urge to selflessly do the right thing.

Whoever the opposing party in your negotiation is, they are also there, just like you, because of the life force that has compelled them, at this point in time, to come to the table. Whatever your differences, you share this starting point.

Abraham Maslow's Motivational Theory: The Hierarchy of Needs

The psychologist Abraham Maslow is remembered for his 1954 book *Motivation and Personality* describing a theoretical model he called the Hierarchy of Needs. His theory remains valid even today in illuminating human motivation in the negotiation process, as well as in management training and personal development.

The Hierarchy of Needs helps explain how certain categories of factors motivate us all. Underlying needs can often be subtle, but Maslow recognized the universality of needs driving the actions of all of us when he wrote:

It is quite true that man lives by bread alone—when there is no bread. But what happens to man's desires when there is plenty of bread and when his belly is chronically filled?

At once other (and "higher") needs emerge and these, rather than physiological hunger, dominate the organism. And when these in turn are satisfied, again new (and still "higher") needs emerge and so on. This is what we mean by saying that the basic human needs are organized into a hierarchy of relative prepotency.[31]

Maslow's Hierarchy of Needs is best pictured as a pyramid ranging from a base of direct biological needs at the bottom to spiritual aspirations at the top.

The Hierarchy of Needs

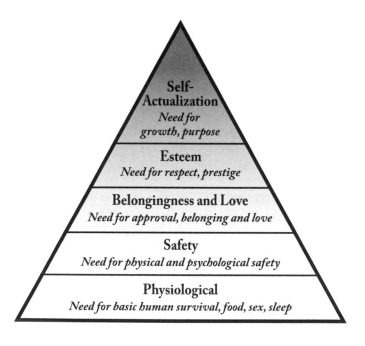

Self-Actualization
Need for growth, purpose

Esteem
Need for respect, prestige

Belongingness and Love
Need for approval, belonging and love

Safety
Need for physical and psychological safety

Physiological
Need for basic human survival, food, sex, sleep

Physiological Our immediate need for food, shelter, rest, sex; our drive to survive and reproduce.[32] As obvious as this fundamental category seems, such needs often show up in our experience in indirect ways, such as the drive to accumulate money, marry a successful mate, or be indulgent or overprotective of offspring.

Safety Personal safety, physical and psychological; the basics of survival extended into storing-up, once immediate needs have been satisfied. Birds build nests; humans accumulate nest-eggs in savings accounts. Here again, the subtleties of our motivation become clear if we consider obvious examples: the elderly "Depression Baby" who hides cash beneath her mattress. Or, for that matter, the "soccer mom" who requires a fortress-like SUV to carry children to the practice field. The need for security also finds expression in our universal need for a *trusted* friend, advisor, or community.

Belongingness and Love Our need for approval and encouragement from family or community, our need to feel we belong among others, our drive to be respected and loved. This category of need often shows up as susceptibility to peer pressure, a misplaced effort to conform to someone else's ideal rather than our own true nature.

Esteem The drive to cultivate a positive self-image or public image, to achieve independence from or lead others, to attain social status, to be revered, to leave behind a legacy.

Self-actualization The need to be what we were born to be, in the highest sense; to discover our personal potential and serve our true purpose; to seek routes of personal growth and peak experience, and achieve fulfillment of our unique individual natures.

We all have different needs that motivate us toward our goals, and every one of them is constantly shifting. Even when we feel we have all of our needs satisfied, changing events can introduce suddenly urgent needs in *every* sector of Maslow's pyramid.

Imagine a family, living comfortably, secure, involved with their community, and active in charitable work. Suddenly a natural disaster, an earthquake or tornado or flood—disrupts their security. Immediately, the family's priorities shift to the *very* basic level: finding food, water, and shelter. At the same time, they also need physical security, a shared love, the support of a community, and a sustaining belief that things will get better. Their need system abruptly reconfigures, and a vastly different new set of parameters applies.

When setbacks throw our plans and assumptions into chaos, an understanding of the universality of needs can provide orientation, a glimmer of light leading us toward survival and fulfillment. Although our circumstances, day to day, are contingent, our spiritual essence inspires us always upward, toward our ideals. Our innate nature is to grow to our highest potential. Yoga master Walt Baptiste said, "These layers of needs are satisfying our instinctive animal nature, human nature, and higher humanity."

Abraham Maslow said, regarding his overall psychological concept of compelling needs, "The specific form that these needs will take will of course vary greatly from person to person. In one individual it may take the form of the desire to be an ideal mother, in another it may be expressed athletically, and in still another it may be expressed in painting pictures or in inventions."[33]

NEEDS, ISSUES, AND POSITIONS

In any negotiation, the process of satisfying needs is the working-out of specific issues at stake and finding resolutions where all parties agree.

What's at stake can be tangible or intangible: a sum of money to change hands, a deed transferring ownership, a time-limit, a boundary, quality requirements, assumption of liability . . . even an exchange of information or an agreement to remain silent and do nothing. In order to satisfy our needs we must deal with particular issues, one at a time.

Based on the issue at stake, we take a specific position: An investment must be examined for X number of days of due diligence; Y dollars must be paid monthly for child support; tolerance for the fit of a product part must be no more than Z millimeters.

We have a need. To satisfy it, there is an issue at stake. We take a specific position on the issue.

A position-focused model brings parties to the negotiation with hardened positions:

Need > Issue > **Position**

What we're learning in this chapter is a need-focused understanding, a reverse journey to a source of strength rooted in the life force that both presents us with needs and leads us toward our fullest realization.

Position > Issue > **Need**

For example, in a divorce settlement negotiation between parents of a young daughter, the individual issues at stake might be weekly visitation rights, monthly child support, and school enrollment. On each of these issues the parties (and possibly their attorneys) come to the negotiating table with specific positions: a certain dollar amount in child support, a certain number of days the child is to be with one or another spouse, the geographic location of the school she'll attend. In other words, everything at stake at this crucial moment has already hardened into specific positions both parties resolutely hold to with a minimum of flexibility.

If, instead, the parents gave their attention to the needs of the child, the negotiation might look quite different and be resolved more collaboratively. Perhaps the idea of setting up an education fund for the child might become a new topic. Perhaps, if they consider that the daughter is in a fragile stage of finding her own identity, the parents might decide she would rather be away at music camp than cooped up Dad's apartment half the summer just to fulfill a legal settlement. During this disruptive period for everyone, perhaps letting the daughter attend the same school as her best friend is a more important factor than mileage from either spouse's home.

Solutions worked out with a fully informed awareness of true underlying needs—in this case, of *all* members of the family affected, not just those at the table—prove more beneficial in the long run than item-by-item jockeying for position. What's at stake at such moments is often a great deal more than quantifiable dollars or days or miles.

As an enlightened negotiator, your job at such times is to explore beyond hardened positions and presumed issues to discover the underlying needs that have brought the parties to the table. Once you're informed and clear about what's required to satisfy everyone's needs, you can then make wise choices that benefit everyone.

THE CONSCIOUSNESS OF AN EXCHANGE

Our very first experience of negotiating, though we're too young to know it, comes when we are infants and toddlers, as we're establishing a sense of self. It's a pure self-interest negotiation. As the life force moves through us, we respond out of sheer instinct, reaching out and grabbing what we need. If someone stands in the way, we press our case with the only assets we have, our lungs and flailing fists and pitiful faces, our ability to make life uncomfortable for those around us (who conveniently seem predisposed toward giving us what we need).

A toddler developing "I-ness," a sense of self, for the first time, will dig in his heels and declare an absolute "No!" as many times as necessary to get what he wants. When we're a bit older and discover total dominance is unlikely, we learn to barter. Two cookies are okay, but there's to be *one* cookie after eating the vegetables and one for putting the toys back in the basket, and a half hour of quiet time for a half hour of "Spongebob Squarepants." If haggling breaks down and there's an impasse, a chaotic outburst such as a tantrum is still an option.

By the time we're old enough to understand the meaning of "negotiation," we're already likely to visualize it in terms of haggling, a wrestling match between our self-interests and another person's annoying reluctance to give us what we want.

This is a simplified way of looking at the different levels of consciousness we move through as we learn negotiation. We begin to develop our ego with awareness wholly of self—*me, me, me*—and gradually develop a consciousness of *us* and *you* and *them*. But as we ascend toward the reality of interconnectedness and oneness, our perspective on the concept of exchange bends more and more toward *enlightened* self-interest and collaboration.

As we saw in the divorce settlement example, parties often come to the negotiation table with hardened positions, a situation that promotes *positional* bargaining, minimal step-by-step movements away from our initial position like plays in a chess game.

The classic example of this style of bargaining is the flea market:

"How much do you want for that ugly wooden figure?"

"Are you referring to this rare hand-carved antique? This must be your lucky day! Because of an unfortunate situation I won't trouble you explaining, I'm forced to sell it for only $100."

"Rare? With all these dings, it must have used as a doorstop. Nobody would pay more than $50 for something in this condition."

"Dings"? It's obviously been kept in an honored place in someone's home. Some polish would restore it to museum condition. But considering the slight wear, I could let it go for $95."

"It looks like my Uncle Harold. I always liked him despite what everyone said about him, so for sentimental reasons I would take it off your hands for $55."

"Well . . . This would be my first sale of the day, and it's good karma to start with an act of charity. If your uncle meant that much to you, I'll let it go at my cost, just for you. You can have it for $85 in cash."

"Here's $75."

This is negotiation as a ping-pong game. Both parties no doubt saw the settlement figure coming from the first volley, and the rest is over a diminishing chance for advantage. Back and forth, back and forth, a creeping advance by reluctant yielding, with no attention given to larger significance or lingering effects.

Naturally, the ancient rituals of haggling serve a broader purpose. In some cultures, the verbal sparring match tests character and builds bonds that smooth the way for future exchanges.

Today, armies of corporate negotiators and security traders are busy haggling (though we don't call it that), over vanishingly small particles of vastly complex deals. Now the back and forth volleys sometimes play out in microseconds in countless specialized languages, formulas, and rituals. Little thought is given to what it all means or why it's necessary in the first place.

There are many resources for learning more about this style of negotiation if one wishes to explore it further.

As our consciousness is moved toward connectedness and oneness, our perspective will shift. We are drawn toward the principles behind our desires, and we look for the source of our motivations. It is from this perspective that we choose what some have called Principled Negotiation, Collaborative Negotiation, Integrative Negotiation, or Constructive Negotiation. More commonly it's referred to as Win-Win Negotiation.

With your awareness of the interconnectedness of all and the totality of your being, the consciousness of enlightened self-interest arises. You move toward collaborative endeavors; you engage in a constructive approach for a mutual gain. You begin integrating additional elements beyond a confined focus and begin capitalizing on unused assets that generate wider resources and more possibilities for creative solutions.

THE KNOWLEDGE OF SELF

We are all familiar with the terms *buyer's remorse* and *seller's remorse*. The dream house seems so much smaller after the sale is closed. The asking price that seemed so ambitious could have been set much higher.

There's also *winner's remorse*. It's not unusual for even the most successful win-win negotiation to leave both parties with a sense of dissatisfaction. Perhaps we've known someone who, after being offered a job they've worked very hard to get, suddenly realizes it's not the right job for them after all. Remember Pamela, the great negotiator, but not an enlightened negotiator?

An empty success happens when we do not have a clear knowledge of our self. Most people move through their lives at a level of consciousness that is clouded, colored, and distorted by countless distractions. We may think we know what we want, purely and simply, but in reality we're subject to subtle forces of envy, misguided ambition, myopic vision, haunting experiences from our past, momentary impulses, or temporary emotional imbalances. It is this disconnect with our true essence that is the root cause of dissatisfaction.

Authentic knowledge of your needs is the foundation of a successful negotiation. It is from here that you embark on the path of negotiation. It is from here that you set your *intention*. This is your launching pad, and any incorrect data built into your calculations will cause a launch failure, a crash landing, or a misguided journey to the wrong destination.

Before you enter any negotiation you must take the time to reach deep within and discover what it is that you need, where the need is coming from, and what practical issues are at stake in satisfying these needs. For example, if one is looking for a job, what's at stake for us? Salary, vacation time, and benefit packages, of course, but what about alignment of the company's philosophy with one's own, the potential for upward mobility, the workplace environment, and location? In other words, that this new role will provide a positive formative experience, not be time spent in purgatory, a learning experience in what can go wrong.

No matter what it is that we are negotiating, whether a peace treaty between two nations or a contract to buy a house, publish a book, or manufacture widgets, confidence at the outset comes only when we are clear about our need-based issues and are able to prioritize them.

Maslow's Hierarchy of Needs can be useful in getting a better understanding of your motivations and assessing whether your core principles and values are congruent with the topics under negotiation—*If I commit myself to the work I'll be doing in this job, will I be moving in the direction my life force compels me, toward my highest self?* If the answer is an honest "Yes," you will enter the negotiations with confidence and from a place of strength. We'll perceive new possibilities, and options will become available to support our forward progress, preventing gridlock and impasse. In the end, seller's or buyer's remorse will not arise, and instead you'll look forward with renewed strength toward the next stage of your journey.

Discovery of the Source Is the Key

Many years ago, I was marketing an estate in a prestigious neighborhood in San Diego. My client, Jeff, an investment banker, had bought the property two years before for $1,000,000. For various reasons, including the facts that he hadn't enjoyed the property as much as he'd expected and he needed to shuffle his portfolio of holdings, he chose to put the property on the market even though the market had slipped and the most that could be realistically justified as an asking price was $800,000.

I was surprised when Jeff, with his acute understanding of markets, absolutely refused to set the asking price at less than what he'd originally paid. He knew and understood our tracking of comparable sales better than most people, but he insisted: *I want to see the million.*

As Jeff's representative, I assumed the duty of what I now call "discovering his needs." But at the time I was simply trying to fathom his unaccountable stubbornness.

It was clear he had fixed his position, like a man with his feet set in concrete, at the $1,000,000 number. The issue seemed to be strictly money (whether the property sold quickly didn't matter to him), which typically signals someone driven by a need for symbols of financial security. But this man was already comfortably wealthy, by any accounting measure, and he *knew* it; this property was only one of many real estate holdings for him. It was obvious to me there were other needs, other matters at stake, that caused the issue of that dollar figure to be absolutely non-negotiable with him.

Maslow's Hierarchy of Needs had been on my mind, and after further discussions with Jeff, it gradually became clear to me that, more than anything else, Jeff's concern was that *word might get around* that he had taken a loss on an investment. Not only would it be bad publicity for his business, but the very thought of having his buddies at his golf club look at him knowing he'd bought a house for $1,000,000 and sold it for $800,000 was intolerable to him. In terms of Maslow's pyramid, he was driven by a burning need at the "respect and prestige" level.

In short order, I sold Jeff's house for him for a $1,000,000 reported closing price with $200,000 worth of "sweetener" for the buyer laced through less-central terms of the contract. (After the buyer's down payment, Jeff personally financed the balance at 4 percent below the commercial market.)

The deal came together because both buyer and seller got what they needed: The buyer got a desirable house at market value, all things considered, and Jeff could offhandedly mention to his golf buddies that, after enjoying his million-dollar getaway for a few years, essentially for free, he had grown tired of owning the property, unloaded it as a "wash" (no small accomplishment in a down market), and was ready for new triumphs.

It was only by knowing the needs, interests, and concerns of the parties involved, including what was at stake for my client at a deeply personal level, that we were able to structure the deal. No amount of marketing or advertising could have sold the property as quickly, without an understanding of the relevant psychological drives.

This is the key, in one form or another, to strength in any successful negotiation. It is only after taking time to accumulate accurate information and develop a clear understanding of what's *truly* at stake that you can move toward a meaningful, mutually beneficial outcome.

Many years ago I heard a man say, "Just because the price of a rope has dropped by 60 percent, you don't hang yourself." This is the best crystallization I've found of a profound and subtle wisdom: Know your true needs and what would be for you a satisfying outcome.

KNOWLEDGE OF "THEM"

As we explore and discover our own needs, our life force draws us up toward an awareness of oneness with all people—the ability to experience the needs of others with empathy.

Often people enter a negotiation with their own purposes crystal clear, but without a clue to what the other side needs. Since the object of negotiation is essentially an exchange of resources (whether goods, services, money, or something vastly more subjective), doesn't it make sense to inform our own position with knowledge of the needs, interests, and motivations of the *other* party in the exchange?

In my years of facilitating and teaching about this subject, it has not been uncommon to hear people involved in a situation requiring negotiation say, "I'm clear on what I need and where I stand. Whatever the other side needs is *their* problem, something I can't possibly know." Despite whatever factors might make such a statement seem undeniable, an exclusively self-focused attitude has never proved to be, in my experience, conducive to an efficient negotiation process or a satisfying outcome.

The more you know about the other side's needs, desires, concerns, and motivations, the more equipped you are to construct an agreement with minimal confusion or friction. For example, for a pair of couples enjoying a night out and deciding among a choice of restaurants, wouldn't be helpful to ask the other party what type of food they're hungry for, what kind of ambiance they would find most suited to the occasion? What's at stake isn't just our *own* tastes and desires, but success in enjoying the evening *together*.

Discovering the other party's needs can be challenging if there's a lack of trust and openness, if there is a gap in knowledge about what one's counterpart is really thinking, if there's a reluctance to "show one's hand," or if there's an assumption that the other party's needs are intrinsically not to be known or "classified" as "a private matter."

However, with time, tenacity, and creativity, openness in this realm can be achieved. After the initial periods of ice breaking and building rapport, you can begin an information exchange by offering some information about yourself and your needs (in chapter 7 we discuss this in greater detail). Once you have set the tone for information sharing, you ask your counterparts about their position, issue, and interest. If the other side is reluctant to respond to direct questions, you could ask "Why not?" or "What is wrong with doing it this way?" This more indirect approach might well give you the desired answer.

Once when I was teaching a course in negotiation, one of my students (we'll call him "Frank") approached me with a big smile and bubbling enthusiasm, rushing to tell me how he'd been successfully applying the principles we'd discussed.

Frank explained that his wife had bought herself a red sports car before they'd met, the car of her dreams as a single woman. But shortly after they were married they were delighted to find out she was pregnant, and a two-seater convertible was an awkward fit for a new family with limited resources.

They'd decided together it was time to trade the sports car for a more suitable vehicle. Responding to an ad, they located a minivan that served their needs, both practical and stylistic. Frank told me that when the moment came to negotiate the sale, instead of jumping directly to the issue of price, but drawing on what he'd learned in my course, he'd asked the seller, "*Why* are you selling this van? What will you do with the money?"

The seller explained that his wife and he no longer had use for a minivan; their children were grown and had moved on to college, and without backseats full of kids, the old van felt downright gloomy. They found themselves using the husband's car, a roomy and comfortable sedan, more and more often.

But then the older man said, "Now we need the cash because my wife wants to buy a sports car! She's always wanted one, but the kids came along and it just wasn't practical all these years." With a mischievous smile he added, "And they say *men* have midlife crises."

Frank suddenly knew it was a match made in heaven. He wouldn't have discovered this if he hadn't been trained in looking beneath the surface.

Not only did the couples swap their cars with no cash changing hands, but the minivan's owners agreed to *delay* the transaction for a few months, so Jeff's wife could zip around town in her red convertible with the wind in her hair, while waiting for the baby to be born. Furthermore, the other man's wife confided to Jeff's wife, "Honey, if caring for a baby gets you down and you miss driving your sports car, just drop by and we'll go for a ride together." Not to be outdone, Frank offered her husband free use of the van if he needed to haul cargo.

A CASE STUDY:
MORGENTHAL FREDERICS

Richard and Leslie Morgenthal are the founders of Morgenthal Frederics, a designer and retailer of luxury optical wear in New York City.

What follows is Richard's own account of a breakthrough in a long negotiation that illustrates how a change of perspective and focusing on the needs of the other party can open new opportunities for cooperation.[34]

> Bergdorf Goodman is one of the premier luxury department store names in the United States. Established more than a century ago, since 1928 its flagship store has been located in what had once been Cornelius Vanderbilt's mansion on Fifth Avenue in mid-town Manhattan. Its parent company now is the multi-store retailer Neiman Marcus; Bergdorf Goodman is the crown jewel in Neiman's high-end retail chain, setting trends with exclusive designers and featuring the finest and costliest goods. For a designer, having its label showcased at Bergdorf Goodman is a crucial milestone, the start of many of leading designers' careers.

As the founders of Morgenthal Frederics, my wife Leslie and I decided early on that developing eyewear designs should be our focus if we were going to succeed. As the designer of the collection, I envisioned products that combined both whimsy and function while incorporating the best manufacturing technology. With our exclusive designs, we succeeded in establishing Morgenthal Frederics within a niche market, distancing ourselves from the competition.

Production of our line involved agreements with our factories in Europe and Japan that specified certain minimum order quantities. Soon, we had more stock than the single store we had at the time could accommodate, and we needed a broader outlet. (By the time we sold our business in 2006, Morgenthal Frederics had seven stores, five in Manhattan in prestigious locations, one in Boston, and another in an exclusive mall on Long Island.)

As a result, we established a wholesale business, selling our collection on a limited basis to select optical retailers outside of New York. We also sold our sunglasses to several specialty stores nationwide, including Neiman Marcus. Shortly thereafter, we were approached by Bergdorf Goodman about our sunglass collection, and we finally decided, even though they were located nearby and Bergdorf might drive down our own shop's sales, that the exposure of being featured by this illustrious retailer was worth the risk. We agreed to supply Bergdorf's sunglass department, and the relationship proved to be quite successful.

Through several years of doing business with Bergdorf at the sunglass-vendor level and observing what the needs, trends, and opportunities were within the department-store model, it grew apparent to me that an even closer relationship with Bergdorf Goodman could be mutually beneficial.

Customer service was paramount to their mission, as it was with Morgenthal Frederics. Bergdorf sold services as well as products; its offerings already included a famous hair salon, a day spa, personal shoppers, custom jewelers, and tailors. I saw an opportunity for Bergdorf to offer another personal service, one that required the shopper to visit the store at least twice: dispensing prescription eyewear, our area of expertise. At the time, there were no other high-end department stores offering eyewear prescription services, and because the idea was unprecedented, we had an uphill battle convincing the executives of Bergdorf Goodman that a viable market existed.

I was clear in presenting my case, focusing on how they'd benefit. Our own products and services catered to a specific demographic that, without a doubt, defined their customer, and just having the service available would set them ahead of their competition.

Over the years, I made many fruitless pleas to Bergdorf's planners for a Morgenthal Frederics optical dispensary within Bergdorf. The response was always that space was at a premium at their flagship store, and they didn't have room for experiments.

Gradually I realized their true underlying concern was that this was change. Our being new designers was one thing—designers come and go—but this was a completely new department in their department store.

From that point on, my goal became to convince the decision-makers, against their primal fears, that a bunch of "doctors" weren't invading their retail operation, but rather the proposal was conventional retailing: Like any other of their upscale suppliers, we provided buyers of our products exceptional customer service.

Confident in the vision of a mutually beneficial arrangement, I persevered through a period when nothing seemed to happen. Then one day in 1999, I received a call from Bergdorf's CEO's office to set up an appointment with me. Within days, the CEO walked into my office with his associate and laid an envelope on the coffee table. He said there was a contract inside it, and he asked if I'd still like to join "our" family. Bergdorf was willing to build a new department for Morgenthal Frederics—out of the limelight at first, but eventually it was moved to the main floor, with signage in the elevators and throughout the store. Soon our relationship with Bergdorf's advertising team confirmed what we'd predicted: They now had a unique innovation in the department store experience, reinforcing in consumers' minds Bergdorf's reputation for quality, convenience, and service, generating continued customer loyalty.

In retrospect, this joint venture grew out of trust, flexibility, communication, clear intention, and the willingness to take a risk. The tipping point came with the realization of the Bergdorf executives' true needs—their reluctance to tamper with a century-old reputation, and their need to stay within the "safety zone" of department-store retailing.

Knowing what is at stake for the other party and how you can bring value to them as well as achieving your own goals is one of the fundamental tenets of Enlightened Negotiation.

THE KNOWLEDGE OF CONTEXT

All negotiations are to some extent influenced by their environments. "Situational awareness," as jet pilots call it, of the real-world context of our negotiation—the time, place, market conditions and competition, as well as industry standards, laws, and regulations keep us from getting bogged down in abstraction and is crucial to structuring a solid outcome.

Let's explore what we mean by "context."

Time The relevance of time is obvious, but sometimes we act as if clocks don't tick and nothing ever changes. If you assume, without bothering to find out for sure, that the hourly rate plumbers charge or the average price of a four-door sedan is still the same as it was ten years ago, you might be in for a shock. Don't make the mistake of living in the past when you negotiate.

Place The price of a muffin is much higher at the airport than at your convenience store. I'll never forget the surprise and amused faces of out of town guests from Kansas (the Sunflower State) as we passed a sidewalk florist in La Jolla, California, a few years ago. The couple experienced "sticker shock" at the price of sunflowers displayed beside roses. Back home, where there are fields of sunflowers nodding to the horizon, no one in their right mind would *pay* for one.

Market Conditions The price of an umbrella goes up when it rains. The price of a typical house is higher when few are on the market. Factual market information, up-to-date statistics, and relevant forecasts are essential for protecting our interests and moving the other side toward a mutually beneficial outcome.

Competition Are you the only one offering what the other party wants, or are there others who, perhaps, are willing to offer a sweeter deal? Yours might be the better product or a more thorough service, but if your competitors are offering discounts, you might have to compete on that level as well.

Industry Standards, Laws, and Regulations It's important to know what steps both parties have to take to satisfy the requirements of institutions outside the negotiation. As the scale of what's at stake in a negotiation increases, so do the legal, regulatory, and tax-related constraints imposed by communities that might be affected. Many transactions get derailed by a detail that's "not up to code" or a document that wasn't filed on time.

Depending on the nature of the transaction, there are likely to be significant checkpoints and speed-bumps along the way: inspections, sample tests, financial reviews, due-diligence periods and countless items that have to be tracked on our radar simultaneously.

Attending to the nuts-and-bolts details may not be the "sexiest" part of negotiating, but unless they're addressed efficiently, the deal may never come together.

There is strength in knowledge, and a crucial category of knowledge, along with understanding ourselves and our counterparts is knowledge of where we are, and understanding the world around us.

SUMMARIZING THE LAW OF STRENGTH

- Your knowledge is the source of your strength; gather information in advance.

- Know your own motives, the underlying needs that have brought you to the negotiating table.

- Know yourself. Ask yourself, would satisfying the needs you've identified be aligned with your core values and higher aspirations? Trust those to guide you toward true satisfaction.

- Process information into knowledge, and apply knowledge with wisdom.

- Avoid merely positional bargaining but rather keep in view broader purposes that serve both sides of the negotiation.

- Discover the same knowledge about the other side of the negotiation, as much as possible. Develop an awareness that we are all connected, and that all may benefit.

- Know your objective, the outcome that would satisfy your needs.

- Negotiations don't happen in a vacuum. Know your surroundings, the context of the situation.

5

∞

The Law of Flexibility

Don't be satisfied with stories, how things have gone with others.
Unfold your own myth.[35]—Rumi

We, as human beings, are biological and organic creatures who are subject to constant growth and the cycle of life. Growth cannot take place without change. Change can be challenging and sometimes difficult or impossible to adapt to. Our ability to adapt to change is called *flexibility.* As the Law of Strength referred to mental strength, in this chapter the Law of Flexibility refers to mental flexibility: stretching the muscles of the mind.

The core of mental flexibility is the ability to see things from several different perspectives, to be able to handle a situation in different ways, and to solve problems with fresh ideas. The mentally flexible person is able to quickly adapt to any new situation and respond effectively.

Cognitive flexibility, by some definitions, refers to the mental capacity to switch between thinking about two or more different concepts, as well as to think about multiple concepts simultaneously. Research has shown that specific brain regions are activated when a person engages in cognitive flexibility tasks.

In behavioral science, mental flexibility is not simply a state of mind or a personality trait; it's a set of behaviors that can be modified or developed. All of us are flexible about some things and inflexible about others, and as we go through life, we modulate our attitudes, becoming open to developing opportunities. When we consider flexibility as "something we do" rather than a fixed part of "who we are," we're more readily able to realize our potential for positive changes and new opportunities.

FLEXIBILITY AND NEGOTIATION

Flexibility in negotiation is the capacity to embrace alternatives without compromising on principles and core values or overstepping necessary limits. In most situations, your sights are set on your goal, and the more ways you envision of *how* to get there, the greater the chance you *will* get there. In a journey from New York to Los Angeles, for example, if we insist on taking only one particular flight that stops in Chicago, offered by only one airline on one particular day, an ice storm in the Midwest could easily block us from getting to our destination. Keeping our options fluid, such as being willing to grab a flight that stops in Atlanta and San Antonio instead, gives us a chance to flow around impediments. One of the characteristics of successful negotiators is this capacity for flexing against pressures that might otherwise cause a breakdown in forward progress. The key is to focus on the goal, not a specific path to it. If our goal is, for example, fair compensation for the job we're agreeing to do, a fixation on the salary figure alone might represent an undervaluing of the compensation package as a whole, which might include educational benefits, relocation reimbursement, or a performance bonus.

A few years ago, a luxury spa resort in California—let's call it Heavenly Resort—had a problem keeping its occupancy rate steady, especially during weekdays. Heavenly had all the infrastructure in place for hosting business conferences and training seminars, and it was confident it had a good team in place to handle the demands of providing a peaceful learning environment. But before the resort could attract organizers of such events such as corporate HR departments, the owners knew they would have to establish a track record.

They decided to develop a training program of their own, publicizing and promoting it at their own expense. Learning of my work with Esalen Institute and training sessions I'd developed for corporate clients such as eBay, Heavenly came to me to develop a series of seminars it could host.

I was intrigued by their proposal because of the opportunity it represented. The resort's managers insisted they wanted the program to be useful, not just an exercise in filling rooms, which set me visualizing favorite topics and speakers I would want to include. The downside was their budget for speaking fees. The owners agreed it was bare-bones, but there wouldn't be a flood of attendees at first, so the resort didn't have cash to spare. The real problem was the empty rooms, but there was no way around it.

The presenters I had in mind had busy schedules and no shortage of opportunities, and I knew that what Heavenly was proposing fell well below the going rate for top-notch presenters. I was about to reluctantly turn down the opportunity, when I thought, *Why are empty rooms a problem?* Why not offer some of the rooms to presenters so they can sell them through their own mailing lists as part of their compensations? Heavenly Resorts may have been short on cash, but it had one asset in abundance: the ability to pamper. If we offered presenters a paid holiday for two that included free rooms and generous free amenities such as spa treatments in addition to a number of free rooms that they could sell—they might be more willing to participate. This would be a win-win for everyone, since sold-out sessions are a boost to presenters' own marketing efforts.

Heavenly's managers were willing to give my proposal a try. I set about planning the series of seminars, and I was able to schedule top-notch presenters who drew overflow crowds.

In the moment I realized that "empty rooms" could be seen as a valuable asset rather than a liability, my mind had whipped from one extreme to another. The very thing that seemed to be the showstopper turned out to be the catalyst for a complete win-win success, but

I could not have visualized this opportunity if I had not been willing to be flexible, to let my thoughts fly from one pole to another. Once I broke away from an unyielding mindset, the fixed notion that the budget wouldn't budge, my creative instincts kicked in. Flexibility enables creativity.

They go hand in hand: Creativity enables flexibility as well.

If you're looking for "wiggle room" in a negotiation or "give" on an intractable problem, it's like trying to unscrew a bolt locked with rust: You might first have to find an alternate path, perhaps by twisting the bolt clockwise instead of counterclockwise, enough to shake loose the corrosion. How else can we be flexible, if there are no alternatives?

CREATIVITY

A mind once stretched to a new idea never returns to its original dimensions.[36]—Oliver Wendell Holmes, *The Autocrat of the Breakfast Table*

A wealthy old sheikh had three sons. He loved them equally, but he also knew they had different prospects in life. His eldest son was bold and knew how to manage assets aggressively, but the youngest was a dreamer who could hardly look after himself and seemed to invite losses. As for the middle son . . . well, there wasn't much to say.

With his sons' distinct qualities in mind, the old sheikh specified in his will that his first-born son was to inherit *half* of all the sheikh's camels, the middle son was to receive a *third*, and the youngest son one *ninth*.

The sheikh eventually died. At the time of his death, he owned 17 camels.

The three sons came together to settle their father's estate respectfully, but the fact that 17 can't be divided by 2, 3, or 9 presented a quandary and soon led them into a heated negotiation, as each proposed a division unacceptable to the other two.

Ali, the eldest, wasn't shy in his demands. "I'm the oldest and the wisest," he crowed, "and I know that our father's wish was for *me* to have all the camels to look after."

The youngest son, Zaleh, disagreed. "Our father knew about my financial setbacks, and he was concerned about my wife's nervous condition. I know that in his heart, he would have wanted *me* to have all the camels."

Mahmoud, the middle son, had enough of their pointless argument and told them, "Most of my life, one or the other of you has gotten all the attention. Ali, you've always been the one destined for greatness, and Zaleh, you were always the precious baby. I was always in the shadows, waiting my turn. Now at last I deserve to be compensated for all the neglect I've endured. All the camels are rightfully *mine*."

At last the three sons decided to consult a village elder, a very wise and very old man who some villagers claimed was a magician. The three brothers explained to the old man their father's bequest and the problem of the 17 camels. The old man listened with his eyes closed and barely showed signs of life until the brothers fell into loudly arguing their extravagant claims. The old man held up a frail hand to silence them.

"There is only one way to solve this problem," he told the brothers. "I will add *my own* camel to the others. Then you will have 18 camels, a sum which can be divided as your father intended."

The brothers protested that they wouldn't think of taking the old man's only camel (for one thing, it looked no healthier than the old man himself), but the old man insisted.

"I'm not worried about it," he assured them. "These things have a way of working out for the best."

The three brothers returned home and added the old man's elderly camel to their father's stock. Then they began sorting their inheritances into separate pens, starting with the least desirable camels to put off arguing as long as possible.

Ali got half of the camels: 18 ÷ 2 = 9.

Mahmud got one-third of the camels: 18 ÷ 3 = 6.

Zaleh got one-ninth of the camels: 18 ÷ 9 = 2.

9 + 6 + 2 = 17.

Astonishingly, the brothers found themselves with one camel left over, the strongest and healthiest of all! This they returned to the old magician in gratitude for his help.

Magic? This Middle Eastern fable is one of my favorites, because it demonstrates the mysterious way even mathematically intractable problems can be resolved with a touch of creativity. All it takes is the flexibility to let go of a fixed idea and extend our thinking to view the problem from another perspective.

To *create* means to bring to existence, first in the mind and heart, and then in the physical world. The *process* of creativity is in the act of setting aside established ideas and visualizing something different and new—sometimes, so radically new that it defies common sense. The *result* of creativity might be a story no one has experienced before, a song no one has heard before, a sculpture no one has seen before . . . or even the solution to a math problem that has baffled great minds for centuries.

Sometimes a breakthrough innovation comes to us so "out of the blue" that we're reluctant to take credit for it.

The idea flow from the human spirit is absolutely unlimited.
All you have to do is tap into that well.[37]—Jack Welch

In many ancient cultures, human beings were not considered the source of their own creativity, but rather only a receptacle for ideas flowing from the gods, as cups receive wine. In ancient Greece, *daemons* were attendant spirits who transferred ideas from Zeus or Athena into the minds of mortals, with the Muses acting as mediators. Inspiration, an act of breathing in, as if it is incense, completes the transfer of this gift. To the Romans, *genius* was the divine entity that gave artists and poets the ability to perceive and capture what other men can't.

DIVERGENT THINKING

. . . it is tempting if the only tool you have is a hammer, to treat everything as though it were a nail.[38]—Abraham Maslow

Ever since humans have come to think of ourselves as the source of that mysterious quality we call creativity, we've been motivated to track the process of creativity to its source. It turns out that exercising creativity, coming up with a new idea, is not the first step in the process. It has a precursor, now known as *divergent thinking*.

Sir Ken Robinson, a recognized expert on the creative process, believes that divergent thinking isn't at all the same thing as creative thinking. Whereas creativity reaches for concepts of practical value, divergent thinking has no relationship with practicality. A defining characteristic of divergent thinking is its eagerness to entertain lots of possible ways of interpreting the question in the first place.

Try this experiment: How many uses can you think of for a paperclip?

The average person can envision ten to fifteen practical things a person could do with a paperclip, but there are a few among us who can easily come up with more than a hundred possibilities. Such people envision variations on the paperclip concept itself, picturing what's possible if you had a paperclip ten stories tall or made of rubber, or if it were a hollow tube. The further we stray from the fixed idea of "paperclip" and toy with the what the question is really asking, the easier it is to envision new applications.

Many of these are absurd and not really "uses," but *that* part of the question is open to interpretation as well. More often than we expect, the best solution to the *real* problem might be something hiding around the bend of a fanciful detour.

The essayist and cartoonist James Thurber, famous for his near-sightedness and quirky insights, tells of his days as an ROTC cadet in college. One day the drill sergeant was in a worse mood than usual and put the unit through a punishing march across the football field with rapid-fire commands: *About face! Right shoulder arms! Right face! Left shoulder arms! Double-time march!*—intended to tangle them up so he'd have further cause to berate them.

At the hour's end all the cadets were, astonishingly, still in perfect step . . . except White, who was marching off at a forty-five degree angle.

"HALT! HALT! HALT!" the sergeant bellowed. Boiling with rage, he ran to where White was standing at petrified attention. The sergeant thrust his finger at White's nose and turned to the other cadets.

"THIS MAN," the sergeant screamed at them, "IS DOING IT RIGHT!"[39]

Divergent thinking doesn't necessarily mean fanciful thinking. It can be remarkably practical. Engineers as well as *New Yorker* cartoonists rely on it.

A number of years ago when digital networking was still being developed, I met a young man, Christopher, who was a gifted software engineer working in a maze of cubicles in a large corporation. Despite the uninspiring environment and layers of approval required for even the most no-brainer innovation, the constant problem-solving aspect of his work kept Christopher's creative nature happy.

But then Christopher suffered serious injuries in an auto accident and was on medical leave for many weeks. When he returned to his office, still recovering, he struggled to cope with the backlog, the projects where he'd been "out of the loop," and the new challenges piling up every day. He knew he could get back up to speed if it weren't for the physical discomfort of his back injuries that made getting around the constrained office environment all but unbearable.

Christopher knew he faced the very real prospect of losing not just his job, but his whole future.

Characteristically, Christopher analyzed various scenarios and possible solutions, viewing the problem from different angles and redefining the variables. He accumulated the best of these ideas— those easiest to implement that would make his situation tolerable, like elevating his desk so he could work standing up—and finally approached his boss.

Each of these ideas the boss rejected out of hand. It would be impossible to get approval. Things just weren't done that way.

Christopher was down to his last idea, the most outlandish: He could *stop coming to work.*

His daily tasks included answering customer's questions, attending team-building sessions and project-planning meetings, collaborative design and coding and document writing, and countless things that come up with no warning. These were situations, in other words, that ruled out being anywhere other than the office.

But was that really true, or was it just an assumption? If there was anything Christopher had learned working with computers, it was that there was no problem that couldn't be solved with wires and bytes.

Best of all, no approval was really necessary. One of the projects already on Christopher's plate was evaluating the security of vendors' data systems for connecting field offices with headquarters. By working from home, he'd simply be testing those systems under real-world conditions.

The boss was intrigued by Christopher's request, so Christopher negotiated a schedule of full days he was required to be in the office and full days when he would be working from his "off-site lab."

Motivated to stay away from the uninspiring environment of the office, Christopher soon ironed-out the kinks and streamlined the systems. He kept his job and became the team's secure-network guru. Today a large percentage of the corporation's full-time employees telecommute or video conference.

Christopher might have been seen as marching off on his own on a divergent course, but in the end it proved to be the *right* one.

George Land and Beth Jarman, in their book *Breakpoint and Beyond: Mastering the Future Today*, describe a study in which 1,600 five-year-old kindergarteners were given a standardized test involving abstract choices developed by NASA to screen adults for creativity (as opposed to intelligence or knowledge), a quality NASA values in its astronauts, engineers, and scientists. Land and Jarman later retested the same 1,600 children five and ten years after the first test.

The results were staggering: *98 percent* of the five-year-olds scored at NASA's "genius" level in terms of creative thinking. Five years later, only 30 percent of the now ten-year-olds scored at this elevated level. When the children were fifteen, only 12 percent scored at the creative genius level. Though Land and Jarman's study ended there, it's not wildly speculative to assume the curve continues until creativity scores level out to the rare "genius" cases we take for granted as adults. (In a separate study where the same standardized creativity test was given to 280,000 adults clustering around the age of 40, only 2 percent tested at the genius level.)

Do these results mean that creativity is a feature of childhood we're all destined to lose as we mature, like baby teeth?

Not really. Aging is universal, but it's not uncommon for even the elderly to have agile imaginations and boundless creativity. There's no direct association.

What Land and Jarman concluded instead was that "non-creativity is learned behavior."

Children are naturally able to blithely sail uncharted waters without fear of obstacles and limitations. They have yet to *learn* the dangers of setting forth into the unknown. They use their imaginations simply to generate countless divergent courses they can explore.

Adults, on the other hand, learn to limit themselves to a narrow and prescribed course of routines and accepted methods, subjecting their fancies to a constant filtering process aligned with conventional wisdom in the hope of minimizing *risk* and *danger*, the concepts toddlers leave to their parents.

The good news is that the capacity for creativity is never really lost. It's always available to us. Other studies have shown we're capable of significantly increasing the number of original ideas we generate if we're given *permission,* meaning freedom and guidance in a secure and nurturing context.

Fostering Creativity

By now you may ask yourself, is this about the Law of Flexibility or the Law of Creativity? Flexibility and creativity are intrinsically linked; it's similar to breath and air.

The essence of the research results described here is that setting free our creativity is really a process of un-learning. Creativity, in spiritual terms, is the free expression of inner wisdom, drawing from the wellspring of childlike innocence before we're beset by phantom inhibitions, limitations, and fears. The primary source of creativity is the Self. In order to foster creativity, we must be able to discover, acknowledge, and connect with your Authentic Self, unconditioned by risk-assessment calculations or circumscribed by boundaries. We rise toward our spiritual essence: pure enthusiasm, creativity, and joy. The true Self exists beyond limiting biases and prejudices and is connected with the whole of which it is part. The true Self reaches out to embrace the unknown as part of the same Self.

Our true Self is not limited to our impressions (and false impressions) of the past. It is capable of transcending our limited experience and of imagining the infinite. In order to cultivate this connection, it might be necessary to re-establish contact with the Self through a regular practice of mindfulness or meditation.

Perhaps the best shortcut to achieving flexibility and creativity is to hang around with creative people. Exploring the "left bank" or bohemian quarter of your communities takes you out of your familiar and circumscribed zone to plateaus of accomplishment defined in unaccustomed ways, from which you can take in vistas you would not experience otherwise.

Cultivating the Aha Moment

The legendary Louis R. Mobley, who founded IBM's Executive School in 1956, had the insight that IBM's success depended on training executives who could, for example, think *creatively* about financial reports rather than merely reacting mechanically to trends and curves and spikes on a graph. As a result of Mobley's research, IBM implemented principles in developing its staff that have revolutionized the field of corporate management.

Mobley believed that creativity isn't an abstract process of intellectual discussion and analysis, but rather a matter of direct sensory experience. His research led him to conclude that the accepted methods of reading, lecturing, and testing were in fact counterproductive.

He set about structuring, instead, a radically nonlinear approach to training. In Mobley's experiments, seasoned and confident executives were put into situations that forced them out of their "comfort zones" into unfamiliar, frustrating, and even humiliating situations deliberately designed to be "mind blowing." Mobley's intent was to elicit the "Aha!" moment that comes to us spontaneously and explosively at the end of a frustrating and chaotic search. Generations of top IBM executives can attest that Mobley's unorthodox methods did indeed prepare them to react creatively to the many challenges they eventually faced.

Negotiating Through a Maze of Unknowns

Creativity is a search into the unknown. You're venturing into unfamiliar territory and feeling your way toward your goal with only the flashlight of your imagination to guide you. Fear of the unknown can creep in at any time, and can't be consciously controlled once panic sets in.

On the other hand, it's possible to prepare for facing a doubtful unknown by envisioning a best-case scenario rather than filling your imagination with dread.

Guided Imagery Therapy is an intervention technique that is often effective for treating severe phobias. Patients are led a step at a time toward the object of their ultimate fears by visualizing the best that can result from a tentative first step, *taking* that step as if dipping a toe in the ocean, and then pausing to calmly assess the patient's resistance and anxiety levels before moving forward.

We encounter examples of guided imagery frequently in daily life. When a corporation introduces its revamped benefits package to employees as the new Family Life-Enhancement Program, we're being *guided toward* envisioning a healthy, vibrant family basking in the glow of regular medical checkups, assured college savings, relaxing vacations, and songs around the campfire. We're being *guided away from* the fear that deductibles have ballooned and the company's contribution to retirement accounts has shrunk.

In negotiation, there is always an element of the unfamiliar or unknown. When the unexpected arises, changing the context can be an effective way of overcoming resistance or obstacles.

The next challenge is to create an environment in which the Self can express itself. Creativity requires a safe and nurturing zone where new ideas are welcomed, treated fairly, and encouraged. In such an environment, uncharted territory can be seen as not only inviting rather than threatening, but also with the pure forward motivation of curiosity and novelty.

Consider one example. How would you negotiate with a child who is fearful of going into an MRI machine?

Dr. Doug Dietz designs medical imaging systems that weigh tons and cost millions. What happens inside them is a miracle of technology, but as a designer Dietz's mission included the machine's outward appearance, the part anxious patients encounter. When surveys of pediatric units using the system began to indicate that nearly 80 percent of their patients needed to be sedated to complete the exam, it was clear the product had a serious design flaw.

Dietz visited pediatric care sites where the MRI units were in use and found cold, echoing environments full of industrial-looking equipment that thumped like antiaircraft fire while the patient, a little boy or girl confined inside a narrow tube, tried to keep perfectly still. He admitted to himself he'd be on the edge of panic himself under these conditions. He couldn't imagine what children would be making of it.

It was clear to him he'd have to expand the meaning of *product design* to include the room, the environment, the sound system, and something else: the *context* in which the patient encounters the machine.

With patients as young as six in mind, Dietz's team created an imaginary environment that comprised an adventure story. Walls were painted with a horizon of sky and sea that included an approaching pirate ship under full sail. A soundtrack played the splash of waves and cries of seagulls, and the scanner was disguised behind a suggestion of crates, nets, and barrels. Young patients entering the unit were encouraged to imagine they were stepping onto the deck of sailing ship with a valuable treasure aboard, under attack by pirates. The valiant captain had ordered everyone below. *There's going to plenty of action up on deck*, the captain had warned—a lot of cannon booms and jolts—*but if we all stay calm and keep still in our hiding places, the pirates will be driven off and we can all celebrate our adventure!*

Shifting the narrative context by turning the scary space of the scanner into the safest, most fun spot in an imaginary scary environment might not have convinced every hospital-savvy six-year-old, but it was enough to replace whimpers with giggles. Within months, Dietz's surveys said only one out of ten pediatric patients in the redesigned units still required sedation.

Giving yourself permission to be creative doesn't work unless you also give yourself permission to be *wrong*. Every good idea grows from the compost of many bad ones, yet the single biggest reason why most of us never live up to our creative potential is our fear of being judged negatively by others.

What we really fear is the stern judge inside each of us who keeps a running tally of our past mistakes and warns us against doing anything foolhardy or potentially embarrassing. Before you can draw on your untapped creative capacity, you have to send the judge away on vacation and give yourself permission to make a complete fool of yourself. It is essential to remind yourself that there are no bad or wrong ideas, only *partially brilliant* ideas that are the building blocks of even brighter ideas.

CREATIVITY IS OPEN-MINDEDNESS

You see things; and you say 'Why?' But I dream things that never were; and I say 'Why not?'[40]—George Bernard Shaw, *Back to Methuselah*

As we come to examine and understand our brains, hearts, and minds we can use our consciousness to alter and control the unconscious wanderings of the mind.

Being creative or artistic doesn't necessarily involve drawing or playing an instrument. Being creative is a way of thinking, a way of processing the world.

Barbara Fredrickson's Broaden and Build theory speculates that positive emotions have the "ability to broaden people's momentary thought-action repertoires, and build their enduring personal resources." The broaden-and-build hypothesis states that positive experiences enable us to have more diverse thoughts and actions, longer attention spans, and wider fields of action, the platforms on which we build the next stage of creative reaching. In one laboratory experiment, subjects were hooked up to sensors that precisely measured the electrical signals of muscles involved specifically in smiling (the *zygnomaticus major*, which draws our lips up at corners, and the *orbiularis coulee*, which causes wrinkles at the corner of the eye). Researchers discovered that when we smile, we quite literally open up, and in that moment we are more receptive and better able to see the big picture.[41]

In another research study, scientists at Cornell University studied the way physicians make diagnoses by asking them to speak their thoughts aloud into a recorder while they examined and diagnosed "patients" (who had been independently diagnosed). In some situations, the patients had been instructed to give the examining doctor a small gift—a bag of candy—prior to the examination.[42]

When the researchers correlated the gift-giving episodes with the transcripts of the physician's thought processes *and* the accuracy of their diagnoses, the results were startling. The physician-subjects who'd been given candy were significantly more apt to think in an open-minded style, reaching out for alternative interpretations of a symptom, and were less likely to become fixed on their initial impression and/or to diagnose prematurely. The accuracy of their diagnoses was also significantly higher than in the cases where the patient didn't offer the diagnostician candy.

At Ross School of Business, University of Michigan, Shirli Kopelman and his colleagues studied the influence of positive, negative, and neutral emotions on negotiated outcomes in a business environment. In one experiment involving a tense face-to-face dispute, negotiators who displayed positive emotions rather than negative or neutral emotions (a poker face), were more likely to incorporate a long-term vision of a future business relationship into their negotiating stance. In a different setting, managers who displayed strategically positive emotion were more likely to come to an agreement and even receive deeper concessions from the other party.[43]

Creating a Positive Environment to Promote Creativity

At the beginning of the year 2000, my wife and I moved to Glen Ellen, a charming little town in the heart of the wine country of Sonoma County and hometown of the writer Jack London. Our home sat atop a mountain overlooking the Valley of the Moon. Trinity Road winds up the mountain through beautiful and captivating scenes, and then a short but bone-jarring dirt road led to our property as well as those of five other families.

Social gatherings in our little neighborhood included grape harvesting, grape stomping, and wine-bottling sessions, which we attended with delight. But we gradually became aware of a deep rivalry and mistrust among some of our neighbors, something with a subtle history. Little by little we learned that the source of this "bad blood" was the matter of the unpaved road. The need to do something about it came up frequently, but every time the group had tried to work out an equitable way of sharing the cost, the discussion devolved into shouting matches about petty resentments from years ago, and everyone went home angry, with nothing decided.

The taboo subject came up one evening when I was enjoying a glass of wine with our nearest neighbor, and he admitted it was a "crazy" situation that had blown all out of proportion. He must have detected my amusement that this one bizarre issue could cause such an amiable group to draw their knives, because he looked me up and down and said, "Why don't *you* try to do it, Mr. Negotiator?"

I took the challenge seriously and started to call around to set up a meeting about having the access road paved. It wasn't a welcome topic, but eventually everyone agreed to at least be present (if only to watch a trained professional fail to get anywhere.)

At our first meeting, as a trained professional I duly set up a flip chart, drew a line down the center, headed the halves *Pro* and *Con*, and invited the participants to shout out, first of all, the Pros, the factors in favor of having the access road paved.

Obvious and logical reasons were offered: A paved road would mean ease of maintenance, reduction of dust, a smoother ride, fewer car repairs. But as the easy answers dried up, I refused to move along to the next subject, the listing of Cons. I kept calling for more and more reasons in favor of the road being paved, until it turned into a party game. The responses kept coming but grew more absurd: "If Joe calls me again in the middle of the night asking if I have extra toilet paper, I could get it to him faster on a paved road."

We were all laughing and trying to outdo ourselves in coming up with silly ideas until we were caught up in an atmosphere of shared play. When we later found our way to touchier matters like apportioning the cost, everyone was able to see "oh-oh!" moments coming and laughed their way back from the brink of "not that again!" disputes with long histories.

Two months later we were all enjoying the only paved "off road" in the area. Word spread to other communities along Trinity Road, and before long a number of other notoriously rough access roads nearby were wearing new coats of asphalt.

Contradictions of the Creative Personality

Mihaly Csikszentmihalyi, in his book *Creativity: Flow and the Psychology of Discovery and Invention*, describes the creative personality as someone with a great deal of energy and a great capacity to stay still.

Those qualities aren't, as first glance might suggest, contradictory. They are instead *complementary* qualities, each incomplete without its opposite.

A sculptor working in marble depends on her ability to channel raw physical energy and emotional passion into hammer blows with both stone-shattering force and exquisite delicacy.

A creative person must be playful yet disciplined. Artists tend to be intelligent and highly educated, but they also often exhibit a child's sense of wonder and naiveté. They're driven by passions and sometimes swirling emotions, yet they must objectively critique their own work moment by moment. An artist is likely to be single-minded in pursuing a vision, but also open to entertaining as many alternatives as possible.

These were the defining characteristics of Lewis Weinberg, the co-chairman and president of Fel-Pro Company, a manufacturer of automobile gaskets and sealants based in Skokie, Illinois. The business had been in Lewis's family since its founding in 1918, and by the time the family sold it in 1998 for $720 million, Fel-Pro had appeared many times on lists of the best companies to work for in America. [44]

"Manufacturing gaskets" conjures up images of gray concrete, grimy windows, and industrial catwalks above roaring machinery. But when I visited Lewis at Fel-Pro's headquarters in 2005, I found an environment as far from that as anyone could imagine. Lewis walked me toward the main building across an inviting green space and pointed with a child's delight to several of the gleaming sculptures that punctuated the lush lawns.

"Gasket manufacturing produces a lot of scrap metal that normally you'd just haul off to be melted down again," Lewis explained. "But that seemed a waste, considering the metal was already in such fascinating shapes. So we set up a resident artist whose job is to create sculptures with whatever he comes across that inspires him. What we don't have room to display here, we offer to the city for public areas and parks. You see quite a few around town."

When we entered the plant, I was struck by the airiness and cleanliness, set off by the colorful abstract graphics painted along the vast walls. I remarked that it must have been a tough decision for the company to spend so much on artwork.

"Why would it be?" Lewis asked me. With a smile of genuine pride, he nodded toward the workers on the shop floor. "These paintings are touching the souls of our family, our employees."

I had come here to learn about Fel-Pro's approach to contract negotiations with the team representing the workers. Lewis assured me the company's management was as hard-headed about dollars and cents as any business, but they tried to be creative about it. When it came to increasing wages, management's philosophy was *What does the company get out of it?* Money given as wages, where the company has no idea where the dollars eventually get spent, was less in the company's interest, they reasoned, than putting the same money toward benefits that contribute to each individual's health and personal improvement, which would make the employee more of an asset to the company.

"We try to *co-invest* with the employees in an intelligent way," Lewis went on, "where both of you get the maximum return for your money. We co-invest in the workers' lifestyle, their health, education, vacation time, and overall morale. In terms of productivity, we have no doubt we got back every dime we've allocated to generous benefits.

In every contract negotiation, we knew we had this golden egg in the room, a valuable bond that management and labor had mutually created and shared pride in, and that sets the framework for a satisfying outcome."

Understanding the Full Personality

There is evidence, surprisingly, that the creative personality might be linked with a *deficit* in mental flexibility.

An April 2013 study published in *Frontiers in Psychology* suggests that people who actually achieve creative success have minds that stubbornly cling to ideas "even to the point where it impairs their ability to shift focus," in the words of the lead author, Darya Zabelina, a graduate student at Northwestern University.

In the Northwestern study, participants were shown images of a large letter made up of small letters (an *F* made up of a pattern of tiny *D*s, for example) and then asked to identify the single large letter hidden among all the small letters. In other instances, the challenge was just the opposite: to shift focus from a large form to identify the small letters that comprise it.

The counterintuitive result was that people who scored high on creativity tests actually performed badly on this test. In fact, they made more than twice as many errors as a group with middling scores in creativity. Even factoring-in overall intelligence, the creative people still fared less well in being able to shift their focus.

The combination of being able to range freely from one thought to another *plus* the ability to focus intensely on a promising idea, once it presents itself, may constitute the "sweet spot" for creative success. The trick is in the timing. There's little advantage to fixing on a single idea when what's needed is as many fresh ideas as possible, or in letting the mind wander once the most promising concept has been selected and it's time to drill into the details.

As we seek to achieve our most creative Self, it's worth keeping in mind the contradictions and trade-offs that might entail. We tend to envision our most creative state as uninhibited and playful, flexible as willows in a breeze. In actuality, creativity might take the form of dogged persistence and an unyielding fix on a precise point on a far horizon.

In negotiation, we hope for a counterpart willing to be as creative about finding solutions as we should be. It's important to keep in mind, however, that a counterpart blessed with a creative personality might also be less willing to let go of a tantalizing but unrealistic ideal, less open to compromise, or less able to "roll with the punches" in an evolving situation.

BRAINSTORMING

Brainstorming is the part of the negotiation process when you harvest the fruits of your flexibility and creativity. When roadblocks arise, you're able to draw on your natural wellspring of creativity and work flexibly with your counterparts to co-create mutually beneficial solutions.

Ralph Keeney, an emeritus professor at Duke University's Fuqua School of Business, has devoted his career to a field called "decision science," helping companies and government agencies bring focus and rigor to their decision-making processes so that less time is wasted in wheel-spinning and objectives are clearly defined at the outset. In his book *Value-Focused Thinking: A Path to Creative Decision-Making*, Keeney says, "Instead of parsing the objectives we hope to achieve, we must direct our energy at coming up with solutions to broadly stated problems."

In negotiation, it's important for us to clearly lay out the problem we're setting out to solve before we can shape the outlines of possible solutions. For example, the *need* for a family vacation, after many months when the kids were busy at school and both parents were working, might be obvious. But what are the real *objectives*? Rest and relaxation for the parents, fun and stimulating activities for the kids, sharing quality time together as a family, alone-time for each individual, and opportunities for exploration and education are worthy goals.

But there might be a number of conflicts about how people want to spend their time and what they consider a satisfying vacation.

Each member of the family has a stake in the outcome, so the first step is for each to offer ideas. A paintball shoot-out might not be Mom's idea of a good time, and the kids might yawn at the thought of touring the Liberace Museum, but how can we know for sure until someone puts forward the idea?

If "two heads are better than one," then the purpose of brainstorming is to engage as many heads as possible. It's essential to start with a wealth of possible solutions on the table, a broad spread of alternatives, from which we can narrow the list down to the most promising avenues of development. Once we have a clear concept of the problem we're addressing and have geared-up to generate as many *partially brilliant* solutions we can think of, we can address ourselves as a group solving the overarching problem collectively and pragmatically with the resources available.

Brainstorming first involves quantity, and then quality. The object is to first gather many points of comparison that can help fill in the big picture, the scope of possibilities. If practical factors constrain the breadth of what you may consider, you can still expand your exploration vertically, like oil prospectors drilling narrow but deep core samples, drawing-in information (whether encouraging or disheartening) to make sure no opportunity is left unexamined. Once numerous possibilities have been evaluated and the wasteful avenues of explorations ruled out, then the search for quality begins.

The cardinal rules of brainstorming exploration are:

Separate the creating time from the evaluating time. It's like a buffet table, no choosing/serving until all the meals are on the table. First put all ideas on the board and THEN start evaluating and choosing.

During the creating time, no judgments. "That's not going to work!" knee-jerk evaluations aren't tolerated, no shoot-from-the-hip critiques allowed; only supportive feedback encouraging even more *partially brilliant* ideas.

No anchoring while creating. It's important to not become fixated on or cling to one particular idea. If "Hawaii" comes up in the first moments of planning the family vacation, no matter how much acceptance the idea receives from its first mention it shouldn't be allowed to overshadow *other* conceivable island destinations, like Ireland or Coney Island.

Brainstorming requires a secure, nurturing environment. Participants must feel safe to present potentially unpopular or off-putting ideas and expose the "divergent" directions of their thoughts. They need to trust that the other participants are also committed to seeking results that will benefit all, and not just scoring points by demolishing others' proposals. Creative solutions require a space for play, and carefree play requires a grounding in trust. Therefore the role of idea-generator must be kept separate from the roles of idea-evaluator and decision-maker.

The second stage of brainstorming shifts us from divergence to *convergence*: We go in different ways in order to collect alternatives, and then we come back together to parse and analyze and settle on a choice that has the best potential for success. In divergence mode we need to be playful and expansive; in convergence mode we need to be focused and aware of limitations. Remember that it is all about the good ideas and not whose ideas.

Dr. Teresa Amabile, who heads the Entrepreneurial Management Unit at Harvard Business School and is the only tenured professor at the school to devote her research program to the study of creativity, believes finance and high-tech sectors in particular tend to be misled by a myth about creativity and competition. The myth, she says, is that internal competition promotes innovation.

In her studies at Harvard, it became evident that creativity takes a hit when participants in a work group compete, rather than collaborate, in coming up with raw ideas. Her research showed that the most productive teams are those that have the confidence to put forward thoughts with the understanding no one is keeping score. But when people compete for recognition, they stop *sharing* information, which is destructive because no single person in an organization has all of the information necessary to put all the pieces of a puzzle together.[45]

ACCESSING THE STATE OF CREATIVITY: THE STATE OF BEING

We are all familiar with those special moments of *Aha!* or a *Eureka!* discovery when the lightbulb appears over our head. It can be as simple as suddenly remembering the name of a Thai restaurant where we enjoyed a meal years ago, or seeing an innovative opening to get past a sticking point in a crucial negotiation. At such times, it seems as if the breakthrough idea *just comes* to us, *striking like lightning* or coming *out of the blue* or *from left field.*

According to lore, as Archimedes was getting into a relaxing bathtub he fell into observing the overflowing water, which triggered his "Eureka!" insight into the relationship between density and volume. Legend has it Newton was resting under a tree when he saw an apple falling off a tree and came to understand the nature of gravity in the time it takes for an apple to reach the earth, and Descartes was lying in bed gazing at a fly on the ceiling when a new understanding of coordinated geometry came to him in a flash. All, according to the stories, were in a state of relaxation before the instant when complex concepts that eluded other great thinkers "came to them," fully formed, in an instant.

However accurate these tales may be, they reflect our common experience, which science has confirmed with the aid of tools measuring the frequency of electrical signals coursing through our brains: A spike of "brain wave" activity associated with the moment loose mental connections abruptly snap together is often preceded by a stretch of lower-frequency electrical patterns associated with meditation and serenity.

Dr. John Kounios,[46] a psychologist at Drexel University, has studied this universally experienced feeling, the abrupt shift in perspective from the train of thought we had been pursuing to a radically new and clear perspective on the problem. Subjects in Dr. Kounios' studies, designed to elicit minor "aha!" moments, exhibited a characteristic pattern of brain wave traces on an EEG marked by a distinctive flash of *gamma* frequency activity, centered in the brain's right hemisphere (the portion of the brain associated with short-term memory associations of objects, sensations, or concepts.) The spike usually occurs at the end of an extended alpha-wave sequence.

"Alpha moments" come as our brain activity transitions from beta to alpha frequencies; as our brains settle into a state of awareness that's calm yet fully aware. It is in this state, research has shown, that we're most likely to have "just came to me out of nowhere" enlightenments. When our brains are active in this manner, in essence our mind is given permission to wander in our vast storehouse of knowledge and experience, to which we have only restricted, need-to-know-basis access when we're locked in the tunnel vision of conscious thought focused on urgent priorities.

When we're awake and performing the normal activities of our daily lives, our brain waves are at a *beta* level of 13-30 Hz cycles per second. In an everyday office situation, for example, when we're filling out forms or checking off inventory, brain signals at 13 Hz predominate. When we answer a customer's telephone call, the frequency rises toward 20 Hz. If the caller's problem is critical or the caller becomes irate, brain wave activity can climb to 30 Hz or beyond.

During a leisurely lunchtime, however, with the morning's problems resolved and a sandwich settling into our digestive system, we may eventually experience the *alpha* level. As we take our brown bag and walk toward the park, our predominant brain-activity frequency drops to 13 Hz; as we enjoy our sandwich, it gets lower still, closer to 10 Hz. After we've eaten and we're lying on the grass looking up at the clouds, the dominant frequency may drop to 8 Hz or below.

When we close our eyes, it dips to about 4 Hz. Below that, we're probably asleep (in the *delta* range) and risking being late for work.

It's in that alpha range from 8 to 15 Hz—when we're still conscious and aware but free of stress, processing different channels of sensory stimuli simultaneously (the buzz of bees, the smell of clover, the warmth of sunlight filtering through leaves) while wandering randomly among diverse and even contradictory intellectual concepts—that we're most likely to experience abrupt spikes of connection-making.

Where you are and what you're doing affects your creativity flow. It's not uncommon to slip into the alpha state during mundane, calming, repetitive tasks (showering, swimming laps, driving a familiar route) that engage the motor neurons governing your muscles, yet leave your analytical minds free from the pressure to judge risks and make decisions. Once urgent matters are resolved or set aside, the mind at rest is able to channel resources into the knitting-up of loose threads, and the creative mind is given a chance to generate fresh ideas.

The good news is that you don't always have to lunch in a park, walk by an ocean, or sit under an apple tree awaiting your "Eureka!" moments. The same level of relaxed attentiveness can also be achieved intentionally through relaxation and meditation techniques. The process requires dedicated effort, but once you come to be familiar with the alpha state, it becomes a reference point enabling us to repeat the steps toward it almost at will. Like any other "muscle memory" skill, like playing the piano or balancing atop a surfboard, being able to direct the body toward the alpha state at will requires proper training and regular practice. To tap into this source of our creative flow with intent and flexibility, you must learn to surf your alpha waves.

Practices to Promote Flexibility and Creativity

The relationship between physical and mental *in*flexibility has long been known. In effect, we store some of the energy of our emotions and worries in our constricted muscles. Physically stretching the muscles and releasing the tensed-up energy, we often experience an associated mental freedom and openness, a flexing of our mental muscles. Practicing yoga, stretching after workouts, and getting regular massages all help our bodies, and therefore, theoretically, our minds become more flexible.

You can test the theory right now. If you've been reading this sitting down, mentally following the steps of the logic and the "guided imagery" of examples and analogies, now stand up and stretch up on your toes, and reach for the ceiling. Walk around your environment a bit; flex your joints and get some blood flowing. Then see if, as a result of this exercise of "letting loose" of this book, (Don't go away, please; we still have much to discuss and discover!) by the time you return, the words you've processed will have taken on playfully different meanings and associations. For example, the word "tight" might have occurred to you if you suddenly flashed on an incident in your own negotiating experience involving a narrow window of opportunity or a "buttoned-down" counterpart. Each time you stretch, try a new way of interacting with your environment and think about staying flexible and relaxed, rolling with the punches, letting go.

How do you best cultivate an internal environment for creativity?

The source of creativity is your true Self. When you connect with your true essence, the wellspring, then creativity will flow forth. It is from that source that you experience your most intense insights, inspirations, and discoveries. From the starting point of your here-and-now daily grind of constantly going, getting, running, and doing, you must journey toward just *being*, toward stillness.

One physical discipline with ancient roots that can lead us toward an aware state of stillness is Yoga Nidra, which in recent years has attracted considerable attention from scientists and health practitioners in the West. Their studies of Yoga Nidra adherents confirms that, in addition to reducing stress and depression and boosting the immune system as many exercise regimens are known to do, the practice of Yoga Nidra also promotes mindfulness and a higher state of awareness, the hallmarks of the brain's alpha state that is the precursor of our flashes of insight.

Yoga Nidra is a state of conscious relaxation where the mind is profoundly calm and yet we remain fully aware. Through the practice and mastery of Yoga Nidra, it's possible to modulate brain-wave activity from the beta level to the alpha and theta stages. Some yoga masters are even able to experience awareness at *delta* level associated with deep sleep. (*Nidra* is the Sanskrit word for *sleep*.)

Mastery of our bodies and our awareness is the ultimate goal of Yoga Nidra adherents, but all of us have a natural capacity to be creative, to be flexible and fluid, and to experience *Aha!* spikes of insight. We can have a reserve of creativity just waiting for us to draw upon it. We can learn from Yoga Nidra practices and begin simply by lying down and systematically relaxing the physical Self. Breathe. Let go of tensions. Grant yourself permission to reach out and explore, and the mental Self will follow.

SUMMARIZING THE LAW OF FLEXIBILITY

- Flexibility is the capacity and ability to embrace change without compromising on principles and core values.
- In order to be flexible you must create alternative options.
- Your true nature is creative but conditionings can inhibit creativity.
- You can consciously tap into your creativity source.
- Positivity promotes an environment for creativity.
- It's important to promote brainstorming in the spirit of co-creation.
- Brainstorming begins with convergence (what are the objectives?), goes through divergence (let's create as many

possibilities as we can), and then goes back to convergence (choosing the best option).

- In divergence, be playful and creative, with no judgment or evaluation. In convergence, be serious, analytical, and practical.

- As long as there is a good idea on the table (during the final convergence), go for it—this is not a contest of wills or of who has a better idea; it is only about good ideas.

- More good ideas mean more good solutions.

6

The Law of Manifestation

Imagination is the beginning of creation. You imagine what you desire, you will what you imagine, and at last, you create what you will.[47]—George Bernard Shaw, *Back to Methusaleh*

We are born to be creative. Our world is what we envision and create collectively. To create is to take inspired action to manifest the result that we want. Manifestation is the transformation of thoughts into a new reality, whether it's a material goal, such as obtaining a house or a car, or a dynamic goal such as getting a job, forming a new partnership, selling a business, or signing a peace treaty. We are responsible for the manifestation process, which dictates the outcome of our individual actions and collective interactions in every moment. Achievement of our desires and goals (our interests and needs) is an act of creation. And negotiation is the path leading there.

We are also creators of the rippling effect that each new act of creation sets in motion. If a family buys a house or a car, they're likely to live a good part of their lives in it, growing up or growing old with it, so the spiritual and emotional consequences of today's choice might well expand far out into the future. There are also people on the periphery who are indirectly affected by the decision the family makes: the salesperson from the company Realtor® or the car salespersons, mortgage brokers, insurance agents, mechanics, and plumbers.

The same applies when a business is sold. Even if the only immediate change is names on legal documents, things will begin to be different, having an effect first on executives, then managers, on down to the field employees and contractors, their families, and the community. There might also be an impact on how customers and the public perceive the business's reputation.

In this chapter we will focus on how best to *co-create* a positive outcome of the negotiation process.

Thus far we've established fundamental elements of negotiation: intention, trust and communication, and preparation. Next we explored our sources of strength and knowledge, and the importance of discovering all information relevant to our current negotiation. We followed with an exploration of creativity as a key to developing flexible ways of achieving our goals.

Now we will explore how all of our efforts are made manifest: How all the knowledge and creativity we're injecting into the process combines to *bring to reality* our clear intention.

This is *show time*. Now we must put into practice all that theory, and make something solid appear.

To appreciate The Law of Manifestation, it's best to look at three key aspects of the concept: foundation, performance, and guidelines.

FOUNDATION

Expectations Drive Behavior

By having high expectations for yourself, you motivate yourself to excel. Keeping high expectations for the results of a negotiation, you prime yourself to be more productive. In addition, having high expectations about the negotiation also has a positive influence on the behavior of the other side, driving them toward achieving higher goals.

The Theories of Aspiration and Dual Concerns

One longstanding model of negotiation is known as Aspiration Theory, and a basic understanding of it should be part of our toolkit. Drawing on empirical evidence, this theory asserts that, participants with high levels of aspiration achieve higher end results for both themselves *and* the other side of the negotiation. As you take the first step on the path to manifesting your intention, you can capitalize on Aspiration Theory by setting optimistic goals for both sides: The buyer and the seller are *both* going to get optimum results; management and employees are going to work and prosper *together*; parents and children are going to live *harmoniously*. There's nothing impossible about any of those futures, so you might as well aspire to them, especially since it's been shown to deliver better results. As Michelangelo put it, "The greater danger for most of us lies not in setting our aim too high and falling short; but in setting our aim too low, and achieving our mark."

According to another long-standing model of negotiation, Dual Concern Theory, negotiators with a higher level of *assertiveness* and *empathy* achieve higher results. In addition, a negotiator who had high concern for herself and high concern for the other party (i.e., had a dual concern) will reach more constructive outcomes.

By now it should be clear that what you are aiming to manifest is what you genuinely believe is the best outcome for all parties. Therefore, our enthusiasm will be manifested through your assertiveness and empathy.

Avoiding Common Pitfalls

There are two common reasons why most negotiations fail:

Parties come to the table with a zero-sum assumption. *In order for me to win, you have to lose.* That's rarely true; there are almost always opportunities for co-creation and collaboration that would benefit *both* parties, if we simply enlarge the scope of myopic vision and open ourselves to new possibilities.

Parties come to the table with fixed positions. For instance they come with a specific salary (though the benefits might be worth even more) or a specific figure per month for child support, (though contributions to the child's college fund ought to be considered). Here again, the solution is simply to enlarge and deepen our field of view: what's being overlooked, what's possible, what *else* would be in line with my needs and goals?

Zero-sum and fixed-position fallacies represent a *scarcity paradigm*, a model of reality based on the assumptions that resources are always finite and possibilities always restricted, a way of looking at the world through a very narrow aperture. As you evolve your consciousness toward Enlightened Negotiation you should already be perceiving the world, instead, as an open field of *inexhaustible* possibilities.

Embracing Common Expectations

When people come to the negotiation table, the very least they expect is:

To be treated fairly. If *you* expect to be treated fairly, *equitably*, be assured that an equal expectation exists on the other side.

To be treated with respect. As evolving human beings, however short of perfection, we all have within us a divine touch that deserves awe and respect. We may not agree with another person's point of view or condone their behavior, but that should never deter us from demonstrating our own best nature by recognizing the other person's.

BATNA

The Best Alternative To a Negotiated Agreement—BATNA—a term coined by Roger Fisher and Bill Ury of the Program on Negotiation at Harvard, can be a useful factor in many negotiations. Often, your negotiating stance is only as powerful as the strength of your BATNA!

Before engaging in any negotiation you must know your alternatives. What if you don't reach an agreement here? What do you do? What if you can't get this new car that's your first choice? What *second* choice would you be happy with?

This should not be a mere rhetorical question—"I'll cross that bridge when I come to it." Knowing your BATNA requires deliberation and research, an exploration of all your alternatives and then analysis to prioritize them. Your second choice should be fleshed out with practical details until you're confident it's not only a viable alternative, it might even be appealing. A strong BATNA gives you the confidence to know when to talk and when to walk.

Narrowing our perception upon the object of this negotiation until we convince ourselves it's the *only* car of our dreams, the *only* house that fits our needs, the *only* vendor able to supply a part, causes us to overvalue it. The more you can convince yourself that this is not an all-or-nothing situation, the stronger your negotiating power will flow as you bargain for that first choice.

General Taste, a wholesale bakery in Del Mar, California, asked me to negotiate the renewal of their lease. My habit, then as now, was to first ask them, "Have you considered other locations?"

Not really, they told me. The idea of moving their bakery operation that included massive ovens, production lines, and a huge freezer, was so daunting to Jonathan, the owner, and his managers that relocating wasn't really worth considering as an option. The lease would have to be renewed; the landlord had them over a barrel. The only question was how much, and that's why they needed a good negotiator.

Over the years they'd been leasing the site in a prominent part of town, they had paid a steady three-percent rent increase every year. During that period, the market had weathered a downturn, which by now put their payments substantially over market rate for rental spaces in that area. Not only that, but the landlord, knowing the company was doing well and assuming its only option for expansion was adjoining floor space he also owned, was offering only a higher lease covering both units.

My clients had hired me to shave anything I could off the rent, not to re-envision their business, but in my many exchanges with the landlord, where I pointed to neighborhood property values making clear his asking price was excessive, my efforts met a brick wall. The landlord wouldn't budge.

When I spoke with Jonathan and the subject of neighborhood values came up, I offered to take him out and show him what the figures meant and I used the outing as an opportunity to take him past comparable locations just across the freeway with a wave of new construction projects. When we looked over the busy construction and the enticing deals being offering in this area, Jonathan opened up with me (and probably himself) about his feelings of being treated unfairly. The steep rent increase was one thing; they could absorb that. But this man's attitude of having control over Jonathan's destiny set his teeth on edge.

As we explored the streets, he began pointing out the advantages an area like this offered the new businesses moving in. We stopped outside a recently built industrial condo for sale, a property a bank had acquired in foreclosure and was offering at a price that hinted it wanted to clear its books quickly. I arranged for a walk-through, and Jonathan pointed out where each piece of equipment could be fitted—and where he'd have problems in his current location.

Jonathan sent me back to the bargaining table with new parameters. The company's most desirable outcome would be staying in place, expansion into the adjacent vacant space with a fair market rent and predictable rate increases.

The negotiation failed. The landlord wouldn't talk, so Jonathan (and I) walked.

With the help of a small business loan, Jonathan acquired the property on the other side of freeway, which gave General Taste more than twice the space it had before at a monthly payment much less than it would have paid in rent.

Once the company took possession of its new space, Jonathan and his managers seemed to take possession of its destiny. The dread of moving heavy equipment was replaced by excitement and a sense of freedom. The company no longer rented, it *owned*. Ten years later, when General Taste sold the property to move its operation to Los Angeles, the profit from its real estate investment surpassed the return from its bakery operation. In the end, its BATNA far exceeded its best-case scenario.

The moral of the story: Don't leave home without your BATNA!

But, as always, don't forget about the other party. At the same time that you're getting comfortable with your back-up plan, you should bear in mind the other side has a BATNA of its own. What do *they* do if you walk away? What are *their* other alternatives, and are those viable? Is their BATNA as good as they think it is?

The home of one my clients adjoined a vacant lot owned by his neighbor. It was a peculiarly shaped lot, but annexing it would give my client more yard space and the possibility of installing a pool the kids had been begging for. When the neighbor was approached, he was open to selling, and I became involved in negotiating the deal.

I considered the current owner's BATNA, his option of keeping the property and developing it himself by building a rental unit on it, and I looked into the details of what that would entail. I discovered that due to local setback requirements and the size of the lot, building a rental unit there wasn't possible.

During the course of our negotiation, sure enough the owner claimed that he was considering building a rental unit on the lot. I pointed out that would not be practical—item by item, I explained why his "option" was wishful thinking rather than something that had any bearing on my client's offer. In the end, the neighbor agreed his options were limited, and my client's kids enjoyed their new pool.

Establishing the Objective Criteria

An important guideline in co-creating an agreement is to assemble your supporting materials—the facts, statistics, case law, cultural background, and objective criteria for measuring results—and understand how inarguable facts can be tools for creating options rather than constraints on what's possible. The more concrete facts you can bring to bear, the more compelling and persuasive your case will be as you strive to bring the other side toward a sense of purpose aligned with your own. In real estate markets, comparisons with recently sold homes in the same category are usually a strong and convincing tool. In negotiating the purchase of a used car, the authority of Blue Book valuations is a powerful tool for establishing an anchor point as our guide. In legal settlements, the judgments in previous similar cases, called precedents, set the standards for defining fair outcomes.

It's important, naturally, to make sure your supporting facts are relevant to the situation, time, and location. For example, the requirements for transferring ownership of real estate properties vary from state to state, and sometimes within a state. Market values usually have strong correlation with time, and in many cases are affected by current events playing out somewhere else in the world. Using information that isn't relevant can lead us into confusion and frustration.

Where there is not a clear standard for evaluation and comparison, if possible, it would be very constructive to co-create a set of guidelines, as demonstrated in the following example:

Nancy, a single mother, was happy to find a good job in a restaurant, but because she was dependent on public transportation she would always arrive for work a few minutes after the opening of the restaurant and have to leave to catch her train a few minutes before the rest of the crew. This liberty she was taking hadn't gone unnoticed by her co-workers. Barbara, Nancy's supervisor, realized that in order for Nancy to arrive or leave in sync with the rest of the crew, for the sake of fairness, she would have to take trains scheduled a full hour before and after the trains she was accustomed to, an almost impossible requirement for a single mother getting kids off to school in the morning and preparing their dinners before bedtime.

Looking at the train schedule in detail and doing the math, Barbara and Nancy noticed that if Nancy took the earlier and later trains *only once a week*, the extra time required neatly matched the accumulated minutes of being late or leaving early on the other days. They worked out an arrangement where Nancy could organize the storeroom or lay out table settings on the one day she'd arrive early and leave late. Once the unusual arrangement was explained to the other workers, everyone was satisfied by its fairness.

This is a small example of co-creating a solution despite outside constraints that would seem to leave no room for accommodation. It wouldn't have been possible if Nancy and Barbara hadn't first assembled the relevant facts by sitting down with the timetables and looking at them closely.

Understanding Human Biases

It's useful to appreciate those general human tendencies that affect everyone's decision-making behavior and judgment, even in the most rational negotiations.

One all-too-human failing is the tendency toward a heuristic approach to problem-solving and decision-making. What this means, essentially, is that we're prone to using mental shortcuts when evaluating complex choices, defaulting to a "rule of thumb" based on what was true in past experiences, even experiences only tangential to the present situation. Ignoring complexities and exceptions saves limited time and allows us to act with some confidence that we have a better-than-ever chance of being correct, without being bogged down in over-analyzing our next course of action. But while a heuristic approach works well enough for many of the decisions we make everyday and often has a reliable basis in truth, it can lead us astray with stereotypes, prejudices, or oversimplifications that have little to do with fact or logic. Shortcut thinking can often prove counter to our interests.

In negotiations with important issues at stake, we must remain vigilant against the human tendency to trust limited personal experience, "everyone says" information, or unexamined assumptions as the basis for wise and safe results.

Another human tendency is the use of intuition. In many wisdom traditions and spiritual practices *intuition* denotes a knowledge arising from inner wisdom and is considered sacred and cherished guidance. In such cultures, the ability to listen for that voice through the noise of our worldly lives and access an inner source of wisdom is a practice that must be cultivated by vigorous training of the mind to transcend distractions.

In modern cultures, however, the term is often used (or rather, misused) to denote a random passing thought that bubbles up in a busy and clouded mind, and has as much to do with accessing truth as numbers in a fortune cookie have to do with winning the lottery. Such "hunches," supposedly rising up from the subconscious or unconscious mind, often represent only latent past impressions stored in our minds and should not be trusted as true perception.

True intuition does not arise in a chaotic mind. It requires cultivating and nurturing. Only through mindful practices and polishing the mirror of our perception can we connect with the source of our intuition.

Deciding Who Should Go First

There are many proponents of waiting for the opposing side to make the first offer at the opening of a negotiation. Their logic is that we learn something about the other side before we've exposed any information about our own position, an example of the zero-sum or scarcity paradigm discussed earlier, the assumption that information must be hoarded, not given freely.

If one is truly starved for information about the object of a negotiation, like the secondhand value of your old computer when you're by no means a "geek" yourself, or the value of that heirloom you inherited when you know nothing about antiques, then, yes, you're better off taking the item to a swap meet and asking, "What would you give me for this?" You're not obligated to accept someone's first offer, after all.

But in most cases, there are very good reasons to go first, to set the tone and focus of the meeting on your own terms, and to capitalize on the power of tools called *anchoring* and *priming.*

The Anchoring Phenomenon

An anchor is a value that serves as an initial reference point: the Blue Book value of a used car, the amount of compensation and damages being asked for when a lawsuit is filed, two weeks of paid vacation as a performance bonus, and a ten-percent customer loyalty discount are all examples of anchoring; they're necessary just to *initiate the process* of negotiation.

What's useful to our purposes is that, when put forth with confidence, an anchor can establish a *cognitive bias* that actualizes the human tendency to strongly favor a known quantity over an abstract possibility when making decisions, even if that known quantity is irrelevant or absolutely arbitrary. This tendency toward nonrational decision making, like others we've already discussed, probably has roots in human evolution.

Daniel Kahneman was awarded the 2002 Nobel Prize in Economics for his work challenging the rational model of judgment and decision making that has long been an assumption of market theorists. His book *Thinking Fast and Slow* describes *two* internal systems that comprise the way we think: System One is fast, immediate, and emotional; System Two is slower, more deliberative, and more logical.

The author reveals the extraordinary capabilities, as well as the shortcomings, of fast thinking and exposes the pervasive influence of our subconscious impressions on our thoughts and choices. In his research on the "anchoring effect," Kahneman and his colleague, Amos Tversky, employed a keno-style wheel of fortune marked from

0 to 100. Participants recruited from University of Oregon were asked to spin the wheel and then write down the number on which the wheel stopped. (Unknown to them, the game was rigged: The wheel was constructed to stop only on the numbers 10 or 65.) The subjects were then asked the following question:

What is your best guess of the percentage of African nations in the UN?

We can all agree that the number from the wheel of fortune had no relevance to these questions, correct? Therefore the participants' answers should have a wide range, since they had no information to go on.

In fact, the statistics revealed participants' answers were clearly affected by the numbers 10 and 65! Those whose spin of the wheel turned up 10 estimated, on average, that 25 percent of U.N. members were African nations. The average estimate of those whose spins turned up 65 was 45 percent. Those "anchoring" numbers, understood by everyone to be irrelevant, significantly influenced the decision making.

In negotiation, the first offer gives the party who makes it an anchoring advantage—the ability to establish criteria or parameters that have a magnetic pull on the opposing party's decision making. Anchoring is effective only up to a certain point, however; one must be aware that in some situations, such as consumer sales of products on the Internet where comparison shopping is easy, or arms-reduction pacts where each nation is well aware of the other's arsenal, a first offer set well outside a known range loses it relevancy and might do more harm than good by signaling an unwillingness to bargain in good faith.

On the other hand, there are ambiguities and complicating factors in the fair-market evaluation of many objects of negotiation, such as a piece of art, a unique product or service, or the amount of punitive damage appropriate in a harassment or discrimination lawsuit. When negotiations center around items or matters of debatable value, even among experts, anchoring the process with a deliberately high or low opening figure—"throwing out a number"—can be effective.

The Power of Priming

Another unconscious influence on our decision-making process is the *priming* effect, which occurs when exposure to one cognitive category unconsciously triggers reference to related categories of knowledge. Kathleen Magian and her colleagues at Harvard Business School, where she teaches courses on negotiation, power, and influence, point out that just mentioning words such as "fairness," "equity," and "mutual benefit" at the outset of a negotiation exchange, even if the words are used in an unrelated context, can set the momentum of the process toward collaboration. It should be obvious by now that as an enlightened negotiator we apply these words in an authentic manner so they set the wheel of associations in motion, affirming a shared belief in fair dealing, toward a mutually satisfying outcome.

PERFORMANCE

Implementation

Enlightened negotiation consists of a set of learned behaviors and skills, some of which might seem alien or awkward if we're accustomed to thinking of negotiation as an all-or-nothing contest. Adapting to an unfamiliar new style and shedding the preconceptions of our way of doing things takes time and patience and may cause uneasiness; you might have the giddy sensation of "going out on a limb." Our negotiation styles are largely habitual and often rooted far back in our childhood.

What is the best way to get rid of an undesirable habit? We cannot simply take an eraser and wipe deeply ingrained habits away, leaving a void. We must replace one mindset with another. It takes time and commitment to replace mindsets that seem as much a part of our identity as fingerprints, but the process begins with small steps, practiced and repeated until they become unconscious "muscle memory." As you grasp the fundamentals of enlightened negotiation, try them out in situations with little at stake, in friendly environments, perhaps with family, friends, or close colleagues before you put them to the test. Then gradually expand your implementation to larger and more demanding situations.

Fundamentally, lasting personal change of any sort involves rewiring our subconscious mind. That requires, first of all, a calm, clear, and receptive state of the mind, which can best be achieved by gentle but insistent repetition (the chanting of monks in meditation is a good example) and visualization infused with authentic emotional commitment.

Rehearsal

Athletes, musicians, dancers, and actors rehearse. Politicians and attorneys have mock debates and moot-case arguments. Why shouldn't negotiators *practice*?

Mental rehearsal helps us deepen our understanding, hone our skills, and perfect our performance. Practicing by role-playing in a context where failure can be forgiven improves coherence and self-confidence. This allows us to organize and fix in our minds facts and figures, and to learn to embody our method of delivery and persuasive attitude.

The late Roger Fisher of the Harvard Program on Negotiation recommends rehearsal and offers a useful tip. When we rehearse what we're going to say, it's natural to play our own role aloud and hear our counterpart's voice in our mind. Fisher suggests doing the opposite: play your counterpart's role aloud. From that shifted perspective, you're likely to feel the strengths of your counterpart's position and hear the weaknesses of your own. Moreover, making an effort to place yourself in the other side's mindset is a beneficial emotional practice that leads to enhanced empathy, an act of defining and refining the kind of energy we want to create and leave behind.

Negotiating with the Right Person

If the outcome of the negotiation is to be manifested, make sure from the outset that you're dealing with people who have authority to turn words into actions. As you equip yourself with information about the other side's motives and positions, don't forget to also assess your counterpart's level of authority and commitment to delivering results. Many negotiations have fallen apart because someone failed to ask in advance, "If we reach agreement, will someone else outside this room still need to approve it?" The same thing applies in reverse. If the negotiation can't be finalized until you've run the terms by your boss or your spouse, you might be negotiating from an uncertain or half-committed position. To start out on solid footing, to negotiate from strength and avoid frustration on the verge of reaching a settlement, it's worth being frank with yourself as well as your counterpart about limitations on your ability to make binding commitments.

If appropriate, should the other side need outside approval, make it clear you can commit to a *tentative* deal, but substantive steps to carry out the arrangement will have to wait.

Establishing Rapport

Creation of the desired outcome begins with intention: A clear understanding of your interests sets the course for your wheel. Exploration of the needs of the other party as well defines the path you'll be traveling from where you are to where you intend to be.

Investigation about the other side should begin from the moment the prospect of a transaction arises. A comprehensive background study of your counterpart, whether he's a housepainter you're considering hiring or a creature from another planet, is likely to turn up useful insights beyond what you're likely to observe superficially in the heat of negotiation.

In any negotiation, establishing rapport with your counterparts is far more than an "ice-breaking" social nicety; it can mean the difference between impasse and going the extra inch to bridge an unresolvable gap on the basis of personal trust. But genuinely getting to know someone requires time and effort and candor.

Many people don't feel comfortable sharing personal or non-public information during negotiation or, indeed, exposing their needs to any degree. Brought up to think of negotiation in terms of a winner-takes-all poker game, many of us equate giving away even a particle of information—"showing our hand"—with giving away everything at stake.

When your counterpart shows reluctance to be candid or to relate on a person-to-person level, you can ease into a state of mutual openness via baby steps, giving freely one opening item of information about yourself, your needs, or expectations, and leaving it to the other side to reciprocate.

For example, in buying or renting a house, there are certain preferences that are general in nature, such as location, size, and number of bedrooms, and then there are specific characteristics that are suitable for us, the buyers. As a warm-up, you can share general information that gives a broad scope of your needs and then move toward the more specific needs such as the layout, color scheme, and landscaping. In this way you are not prematurely revealing all information at once—although the ultimate goal is to be fully open.

We should bear in mind that negotiation is a labor of *co-creation* that requires, at the very least, honest engagement of the parties involved and, at best, brings them together to work in unison, in a true collaboration. From a spiritual perspective, the wholeness of the enterprise takes shape, to have a single outcome with many facets serving differing purposes. In even the most quarrelsome situation, despite what logic or our own emotional impulses might tell us, taking the time to explore the needs, emotions, and thought processes of the other side aligns our labor with natural forces already at work in a universe in which everything is ultimately connected. Providing the other party with as much benefit as possible without jeopardizing our own needs is seldom, if ever, impossible if we use our imaginations and our capacity for empathy.

For example, the decision of the Allied leaders to leave the Japanese emperor on his throne after Japan's defeat in the Second World War, when it was crucial to the victors to avoid any appearance of negotiation with an enemy that had surrendered *unconditionally*, was a gesture that advanced the world's overarching need to consign the evils of the war to the past and move forward in peace. In acknowledging the Japanese people's complex emotional and spiritual ties to their cultural identity, it laid a foundation of mutual understanding and respect that—beyond even the optimists' hopes—eventually turned a bitter, humiliated enemy into a close friend and ally.

Manifesting our dreams in the physical world requires methods we don't normally associate with hard-headed bargaining; among them are the willingness to give information freely, an understanding of our counterpart's needs and motivations in addition to our own, and a sincere commitment to labor *alongside* the party across from us toward a solution that will benefit even diametrically opposed interests.

Let's continue to explore some other often overlooked but remarkably useful methods of Enlightened Negotiation.

Centering

Once you've taken the time to establish in advance your own intent as you set out to accomplish your goals, it's extremely helpful to do the same exercise jointly with your counterparts when commencing negotiations. Forming together a clear joint intention harmonizes the unified field of your separate minds toward creation of an optimum manifestation. Whether you're engaged in a business exchange, in defining and implementing public policy, or simply deciding as a family where to go on vacation, a surprisingly powerful practice is to start the meeting with a moment of silence and stillness. After all, if we can't tolerate simply sitting together in silence for a couple of minutes, how we can tolerate listening to each other and working together?

Some people don't feel comfortable with conspicuous silence, and in such cases you might want to frame the concept differently. You can ask, "Before we get down to issues, can we all take a moment to collect our thoughts?" or "May I invite everyone to participate in a 'centering' exercise that won't take more than a minute and might help us get off to a good start?" Explain that it's not magic or mumbo-jumbo; reflecting on the goal of a process at its outset and visualizing a successful conclusion has been shown to increase productivity and save time and effort in the long run.

If you're the one proposing a moment of silence and centering, it's worth experimenting with the practice in advance. You should feel comfortable with silence yourself before you recommend it to others, and it's necessary to have an awareness of being centered and composed to have the confidence to draw in someone who might not be accepting of unconventional methods.

PRESENTATION

This presentation stage is the heart of any negotiation process. This is where all of your efforts in preparation, information gathering, analyzing, and planning come together. This is where you begin to move toward manifestation of an eventual agreement, putting forth your position with words, tone, and body language that express your intention. As in most things, the first impression you make shapes everything that comes after and can't easily be replaced.

Changing someone's mind takes a lot of effort, points out Nobel Laureate Daniel Kahneman. Like the locomotive of a train, your opening must be powerful enough to overcome inertia and wheel spinning to move you forward from a dead stop.

In your presentation, be sure to review the objectives: yours and theirs. The checkpoints that measure our progress, the milestones along the way. Make sure you are concise and clear about the ultimate mutual goals and the steps necessary to realize them.

Now look for a first "yes," an opportunity to reach initial agreement—on anything! Addressing even minor issues and reaching agreements on them creates forward momentum that helps carry us toward reaching agreement on more complex and significant issues.

As you proceed, turn the discussion to envisioning how a possible agreement would reflect the goals and measurements of the objectives, then build on the initial "yes" and each point of agreement by confirming them and avoiding back-tracking. Like a rock-climber moving from foothold to foothold, seek out existing points of partial agreement as the basis for reaching out toward the next, so that consensus develops in an organic, natural way.

At the end of any negotiation session, recap the progress of the meeting, even if the ultimate goal seems no closer. Acknowledge what has been achieved and confirm the process is on the right path. Then clarify the next steps in the process and the action plan for addressing them.

The Embodiment Principle

As we discussed earlier, our message is conveyed through many means beyond the words that we use. Beyond what we say, our posture and tonality communicate our emotions and our level of confidence.

The mind-body connection is a bidirectional system. Our thoughts affect our bodies, and how we hold our bodies affects our thinking. Dr. Amy Cuddy, a social psychologist and associated professor at Harvard Business School, studies the origins and outcomes of the way we perceive and are influenced by other people on a non-verbal level, investigating the subtle roles of stereotypes, emotions, physical behaviors, and even hormones. Cuddy's research with Dana Carney[48] of U.C. Berkeley largely focuses on how nonverbal expressions of power (e.g., expansive, open, space-occupying postures) affect people's feelings, impulses, and hormone levels. In particular, the research shows that assumed body postures associated with dominance and power ("power posing")—even for as little as two minutes—increases subjects' testosterone levels (associated with dominance, competition, and winning), decreases cortisol (a stress hormone), increases their appetite for risk, and causes them to perform better in job interviews.

What's remarkable is that we don't need to assume power poses at the negotiation table to trigger the positive effects; just preparing oneself in advance by holding expansive poses with no one watching can instill a can-do attitude in us. What's more, it doesn't require us to use inauthentic or intimidating signals (which can be unconvincing to someone who's read the same books on body language).

Try interlacing your fingers behind your head with your elbows pushed back, legs wide, and chest thrust out. Stretch and reach out for the world. If you practice yoga, you may want to hold the warrior pose. Once you act powerfully, you will begin to think powerfully.

Remember, since you're cultivating collaboration and co-creation, your sense of power is meant to be shared for a mutual win-win benefit, not deployed to overpower or threaten an adversary.

Balancing Act: Gentle on the People, Hard on the Message

It's good to remember we can often be flexible about minor issues, but we mustn't yield on core principles.

Here is a conversation I once witnessed between a school principal and the school bus driver:

"Mr. Jackson, at Wisdom High School we are proud of our success in graduating students with a firm foundation based on two core principles: discipline and tolerance. You're a valuable member of our staff so we've shown sensitivity and flexibility about your recent personal challenges, leniency about your absenteeism, and generosity in your benefits. But, as you know, there's zero tolerance about anything that might jeopardize the safety of the children in our care. So please consider any driving violation citation your pink slip."

Written Words

Since negotiation is an exchange between humans, it's natural to assume that negotiating face-to-face is the most efficient way. However, in today's technology-rich environment, many people opt for written negotiation for the sake of time, convenience, and also clarity. It's unproductive to deny the value of written communications, by email or even text messaging, just because we fear writing is too cold or impersonal.

In writing, you have the luxury of composing your thoughts at your leisure and then crafting a precise message, drawing on the information and knowledge you've assembled. You have the option of editing whatever you've written, if you have second thoughts, rather than being committed to whatever words pop out of your mouth on the spur of the moment. You can prioritize items and fine-tune your words to be as powerful and persuasive as they can be.

Opening a negotiation with written notes allows you to perfect your initial presentation, make use of priming and anchoring gambits, and sets a tone leading toward an integrative approach. You can then switch to face-to-face, (I mean side-by-side) extemporaneous communication when the situation calls for it.

It's the Package, Not the Pieces

The final agreement of most negotiations tends to come as a package or bundle. Although we dissect and discuss issues one by one, the goal is the *totality* of the agreement. It's useful for both parties to make clear at the beginning of the process that there is no deal until *all* issues have been addressed and agreed to, and the necessary actions to fulfill the agreement are set in motion.

Any changes in one issue might necessitate modification in other settled issues, and sometimes it's not possible to make everything invariable, chiseled in stone. Let's say you've agreed on price, quality, and time of delivery of parts for a product. A change in delivery time could impact the price or quality, or both. "If/then" language should be used to address this kind of contingency. For example, "*If* you require rush delivery with the same quality, *then* the price would be X; *if* you need rush delivery at the same price, *then* we will have to cut corners on quality."

GUIDELINES

A nice guy doesn't mean . . .

There is a well-known story in the Vedas, the ancient Hindu scriptures, that contain hymns, philosophy, and also sly practical advice.

A traveling sage was passing through a village to spread his teachings and came across an enormous, menacing snake that had been terrorizing the townspeople. The sage addressed the snake as if it were his student, and taught it the first principle of righteous living: non-violence or *ahimsa*. The snake was touched by the teaching and took it to the heart.

The following year, as the sage was making his yearly circuit through the area, he again encountered the snake and was surprised to see it in terrible shape. This once magnificent creature—strong, alert, vigorous and vibrantly colored—was now skinny and bruised and sickly. The sage asked the snake what had happened.

The snake replied that he had practiced ahimsa by stopping his terrorizing of the villagers. But because he was no longer menacing, the children now threw rocks at him and taunted him. He added that he was afraid to leave his hiding place to hunt for food.

The sage shook his head. "Indeed I did advise against violence," he told the snake. "But I never told you not to hiss."

Protecting yourself and others does not violate ahimsa. Practicing ahimsa certainly means you refrain from your own harmful behavior and do your best to prevent others from causing harm. But being passive is not the point, and it is not the full practice of ahimsa. True ahimsa flows from your true nature, and nature provides you with everything you need to stand up for your rights without violence.

Tit for Tat

In general, it's beneficial to promote cooperation and collaboration; however, when a counterpart insists on behaving selfishly or irrationally, a cooperative strategy might not sustainable. In other words, no one wants to be a sucker. That is when a not so childish "tit for tat," a mirror in which our counterpart will see himself, may be the only option to draw the other side into understanding our point of view and, hopefully, seeing how our interests reflect his.

One day I ran into my friend Mary at a coffee shop, sitting by herself and busy as always tapping and talking on her phone. She told me she was waiting for her customer Roger to arrive and finalize an order for the uniforms made by her company. She invited me to sit down while I waited for my order.

She asked me about something going on in my life, but I said, "I'll tell you the whole story when you have more time."

"Tell me now," she said. "Roger is *always* twenty minutes late. The annoying thing is, he doesn't realize how annoying it is."

Eighteen minutes later, Mary pointed out a man getting out of his car and leisurely walking toward the coffee shop. As we watched Roger stand at the counter and place his order, Mary pulled out her cell phone and called her secretary. "Call me back in exactly one minute," she told her.

Roger walked over to our table and Mary introduced us, and Roger casually remarked that he'd been delayed by something that had come up.

"No problem!" Mary said. "Mehrad and I got a chance to catch up."

Just then, her phone rang.

"Roger, I have to take this call. Something's come up. Why don't you and Mehrad get to know each other? This should only take about twenty minutes."

I excused myself quickly, explaining my wife was probably already waiting at our car. The *real* reason was that I was afraid I'd explode with laughter, and I walked away wondering if Mary would keep Roger in her penalty box for the full twenty minutes. I have a feeling she did.

Characteristically, Mary made her point in a demonstrative way, and I have no doubt Roger got her message. She had been flexible and understanding enough, but we all need to draw the line sometimes.

Mary was demanding respect for herself and her time, just as Roger would.

How Much Do You Want IT?

In my negotiation class I sometimes take out a $20 bill and walk along the front row of students, holding the bill out to them just beyond their reach.

I ask the class, "Who *seriously* wants this $20, no strings attached?" Most students raise their hands, although some hold back, sensing I might have hidden motives.

Then I ask, "Who *sincerely* wants this?" This time I see everyone's hands in the air, and some people raise both hands.

Usually, before I asked any more questions probing how deeply they want the free money, someone walks up to me, takes the $20 bill from my hand, pockets it, and returns to his seat.

At that point, everyone catches on and laughs.

If your desire is authentic, you then have to act! What's holding you back? If a negotiation is bogged down in talk at the verge of consummation, take the initiative and *act*. Break the inertia by demonstrating how easy it is for the other side to cover the last few inches that separate you.

Don't Play the Losing Game

There are instances where we've invested time and money in a situation but then realize it's a losing scenario for us. In order to "protect" our investment, however, we keep playing the losing game anyway, doubling-down on wasted effort. Obviously, this is not a wise course.

The moment we discover a negotiation is unlikely to serve our interests and is wasting resources, it's best to accept our loss and move on.

In my negotiation course, we sometimes play a bidding game where the successful bidder pays only the amount he's raised the bid above the previous bidder's, and the last unsuccessful bidder is responsible for paying the balance. For example if Bidder A offers $18 and bidder B bids $20, and there are no more bids, then B pays only $2 and A pays $18.

I begin by holding up a $20 bill being auctioned, with a minimum bid of $1 required. Of course it's tempting to start bidding—$19 in quick profit? Why not?—but the trick is that once you start playing, you have to continue to play to avoid being the next-to-last bidder who doesn't take home the prize but has to pay out his bid anyway. Avoiding loss quickly becomes more important than achieving gain, and the spectators watch in amazement as the bidding climbs *above* $20!

The point is that our sometimes irrational need to avoid writing off a loss can be more powerful than the rational desire for gain.

Avoid Traps

There are many ancient ploys and tricks that some people aren't above using to tip a negotiation to their advantage unfairly. These include deliberately supplying false information, using psychological pressure tactics (like the familiar good cop/bad cop tactic of police interrogations), stonewalling, or unreasonable delays. In order to avoid these traps first you must recognize them and then bring them out into the open. A ploy recognized is a ploy disarmed.

Stay on Track

It is essential to remember that our goal is to *manifest* what we want and make it a reality, not a "might have been." That is our guiding light. Assuming that by the time we begin our presentation our intention is clearly set, the systematic approach is to put it in motion, beginning with the discovery of everyone's compelling needs and then co-creatively generating as many routes to an agreeable solution as we can imagine. We continue by nailing down partial agreements in draft form, fine-tuning the details, and eventually *executing* what has been agreed to rather than leaving it half-realized. It can be a long journey, and it's easy to wander off the path of progress either unintentionally or, sometimes, from the other side's intent to reopen issues that have been settled. Stories, memories, asides and digressions can be helpful up to a point, by building rapport when consensus is elusive, but they can also be distracting. Even statistics and formulae that are essential for the process of negotiation can bog down progress and make agreement seem unattainable. If your counterpart is going off on a tangent, simply remind him or her that, although you would like to know more, those topics can be addressed later but this moment is for moving forward productively.

A few years ago, I was dealing with a foreign company whose CEO was remarkably receptive to most of the items proposed in a complex deal; her goal was clear in her mind and she was eager to move toward it with a minimum of roadblocks. All that remained was to meet with a manager reporting to the CEO to iron out logistics.

I had met the manager before and had good rapport with him, and in our meeting he cheerfully shared unrelated personal experiences in considerable detail. Unfortunately, I had a plane to catch, and by the end of the time we had available, we hadn't covered more than one or two items on our crowded agenda, so we scheduled a phone conference to follow up on the rest.

Over the phone, I noticed the same pattern of endless small-talk developing, and the more I tried to steer the conversation back to the subject at hand, the more resistant the manager became to my reminders we had work to accomplish. In probing indirectly, I became aware of a subtle hostility being masked by his show of warmth and comradeship—in truth, he was not wholeheartedly supportive of the program the CEO and I had put together. Furthermore, I learned he had an underlying fear that the program would be a success. Although it was a good plan benefiting the whole organization, this manager perceived it as a threat to his security, simply because it hadn't been his idea originally and someone else would get the credit.

Although I was hoping for a smooth path to implementation once the plan had the CEO's blessing, the reality of the situation was quite different from what it seemed. Internal rivalries split the organization, and the CEO's show of decisiveness was neutralized at every step by the cheerful passive resistance of his subordinates. Every "of course" and "I agree" and "I'll take care of it right away" was in fact a vow to derail the project.

Don't Burn Your Bridges

Not all negotiations result in an agreement. Just because you're a skillful negotiator you're not guaranteed to walk away with everything you want. Even with all the wisdom we discussed so far, we must recognize that there are still situations we cannot resolve, and we have to move on. Sometimes the most we can accomplish is to learn from the failure so we can strengthen our performance next time.

What do we say to our counterpart when this happens? The best thing is to say, simply, "This doesn't seem to be a good time to work together, but I look forward to other opportunities in the future." It's best to neutralize personal issues by pointing to external economic or physical issues that just don't make agreement practical.

The worst thing you can do is end the process with animosity.

There's no need to slam the door on your way out. Instead, sincerely wish the other party well and leave the door open for a healthy relationship that might lead to progress next time.

A CASE STUDY:
THE SALE OF THE KASHI COMPANY

What follows is the story of the sale of Kashi Company, an internationally recognized brand of healthy, natural breakfast cereals and grain-based foods.

Philip and Gayle Tauber, colleagues and dear friends of mine, started Kashi in the early 1980s. By the time Kashi established itself as a dominant brand in the health-food market, several giant cereal companies who saw opportunities in the same market decided it made sense to acquire an established client base and solid name recognition by buying an existing company. Two dominant players in the breakfast cereal market, Kellogg's Company and Kraft Foods, were both interested in acquiring Kashi.

To its owners, the sale of the company was more than just a sale to its new owners, Philip emphasized. "In going into the negotiation, I was aware first of the fact that I was negotiating, and not simply in the midst of 'selling' something. That was a very important distinction for me."

Here is Philip and Gayle Tauber's story:[49]

> In the later part of 2000, both Kellogg's and Kraft Foods called to inquire if Kashi might be open to selling part of the company through an equity stake of some sort. Gayle and I discussed the conditions under which either of those options might be possible—first, what might be the best outcome for the company, then what would be best for ourselves and our employees. Preserving the brand we'd built, and how any agreement might impact loyal consumers of the brand, also factored heavily in our thoughts.
>
> We really hadn't much interest in selling the company until these two giant corporations called us within a few weeks of each other. Knowing that we were in a growth phase and on the point of launching what would be a gigantic leap forward for us—the Kashi Go Lean line of meal replacements, energy bars, shakes, cereals, and ready-to-serve on-the-go meals—we faced a conundrum. We thought this line would increase our value vastly. But since we had no track record of sales for the new products, we were hard-pressed to determine how much value this additional revenue generator would add to the existing core products.
>
> We were ready to grow into national and international distribution, but that would require many millions

of dollars in marketing and advertising. The major players in the industry not only understood this as well as we did, they had the advantage of being able to throw up roadblocks in our sales channels with the clout of their sales forces, making it difficult for us to get the shelf space in the supermarkets we would need to even begin a consumer push.

The writing was on the wall: Raise capital through private placement, go public, or sell. We decided to sell, even though we thought the timing was a bit premature for us as a company, but right because having corporate giants fight over us represented an opportunity that might not ever come again.

Our meetings were held in a small hotel space where each company represented its interests through their corporate acquisitions team, lawyers, and corporate officers. Gayle and I, with only the assistance of our one attorney, sat and listened to the pitches.

Both companies put forth every reason why we should sell, telling us how well we would do personally, what the future of the company might look like after the sale, and what our own roles would be going forward. We listened and learned, hardly speaking at all.

Both companies seemed trustworthy and respectful toward us, and yet there was this underlying attitude of "we're bigger, so we know best," as if the negotiating table already tilted in their direction.

They were big, rich, and powerful, but they also very badly wanted something we had. We knew to hold tight to our core values, our vision of where we were going, and our desires for a fruitful outcome. It's not all about money, we decided. Our employees and our reputation also mattered to us very deeply.

That gave us an inner peace. I would describe this feeling as a positive "comfort of knowing" and valuing our accomplishments, rather than a pumped up ego at being courted, or a misguided sense of entitlement.

In the decision between our two suitors, it came down to these points:

- ° Kraft offered substantially more than Kellogg's in money, but would incorporate the brand into one of its existing lines. It would lay off our staff, and move our facility to Tarrytown, New York. The founding ideals and heritage of the company we'd built would vanish and be replaced by Kraft's.

- ° Kraft was owned by the giant tobacco company Phillip Morris, whose products were anathema to our core values of a healthy life style.

- ° Kellogg's saw no problem with keeping the company in La Jolla, California, where it originated, and intended to retain the entire present staff and operations. It saw value in preserving the Kashi brand and health-conscious image, and was ready to invest millions of dollars in advertising and marketing to extend that image. Moreover, we felt they were treating us like equals, understanding that they'd have to further negotiate terms that everyone could live with.

Kraft, on the other hand, assumed it was already a done deal, which made our decision easy: Our choice would be Kellogg's.

In hindsight, I think the negotiation hinged on which company might better represent our interests. Knowing the outline of the working sentiments of both parties, we settled the finances and the terms and conditions of the transfer quite easily. The terms of sale were worked out collaboratively, with both parties having a good deal of understanding about the other's needs.

In the end, an all-cash price was settled on instead of a mixed or all-stock buyout. Both Gayle and I were retained by the new owners, and our contracts ensured we would have roles influencing the direction of the brand for at least several years after the sale. We all felt the employees should share in the good fortune, so the employees were all granted shares of Kellogg's stock, plus cash bonuses, and promised performance reviews leading to promotion opportunities. Kashi's involvement in social responsibility and venture-capital efforts would be continued, and our loyal consumer base would be treasured.

Because it wasn't all about the money, we settled on a reasonable price for the core brand with a track record of sales, and were allowed a stake in the future of our planned Go Lean line if it proved profitable. Kellogg's accounting team worked out a milestone-marker tool that gave us three years of bonus payments if the target goals for the Go Lean line were reached. As it turns out, the goals were exceeded, and they paid us well!

Some people think we sold too soon, others told us we should have gotten more money, and quite a few thought we should have kept the company. But truth be told, we're very happy to see the brand thriving and the healthy-food market expanding, and that means more to us than money. We were very pleased with the settlement, and Kellogg's has been remarkably responsible in carrying-through the commitments it made. Of course there have been some bumps in the road, issues concerning leadership and execution, but for the most part, we are proud of the brand, its mission, and its future.

I'm happy to report that the "negotiations in advance of the negotiations" proved to be the secret of this successful transition.

In this case study the parties had clear intention, trusted each other, communicated clearly, had full knowledge, practiced flexibility, and were mindful of each other, the larger context, and the process. By the time negotiations over price and terms got underway, they already had a thorough understanding of each other's needs and had tentatively agreed to basic elements. When it came time to settle the details, the parties were able to zoom-in on creative solutions efficiently and speed to a close.

The outcome unfolded in accordance with The Laws of Enlightened Negotiation we've discussed so far, and everything desired was manifested.

SUMMARIZING THE LAW OF MANIFESTATION

- Manifestation is "show time."
- Avoid the common pitfalls.
- Embrace the common expectations.
- Negotiate with the right person.
- Begin with centering.
- Use the power of anchoring and priming.
- Establish our objective criteria.
- Know when to talk and when to walk. (BATNA)
- Stay on track.
- Be aware of the tricks and call them.
- Start drafting your agreement early.

7

The Law of Mindfulness

*A human being is a part of the whole, called by us "Universe,"
a part limited in time and space. He experiences himself,
his thoughts and feelings as something separate from the rest—
a kind of optical delusion of his consciousness.*[50]—Albert Einstein

Mindfulness is not a word most people use in everyday conversation. When you hear it, what does your mind conjure? A Zen follower in meditation? A woodworker running a power saw? What are we being mindful *of*?

Where we are?

The present moment?

What we're doing?

Let's make it simple. When we're mindful of our true essence, our authentic self or our higher self, *all of the above* are involved. We will be aware of time, space, our feelings, our bodies and physical movements, and our conscious thoughts. We don't need to go through a checklist.

Mindfulness in enlightened negotiation is about mindfulness of Self, mindfulness of others, and mindfulness of the creative process. Negotiation requires the convergence of two or more parties toward a collectively satisfactory agreement. People must deal with people. Regardless of how you master all other elements and follow the other principles of negotiation, the ultimate test of your success is how you deal with *people*.

UNDERSTANDING PEOPLE

People will forget what you said. People will forget what you did. But people will never forget how you made them feel.[51]

—Maya Angelou

Mindfulness in any negotiation involves awareness that behind any name, face, voice, title, or signature, there is a unique human being, a Self. In order to understand others we must have clear vision; we must clean our lenses and remove any haze or distortion between us.

Picture a modern ballet: The lights go up and first you see the dancers as abstract shadows moving behind layers of shifting curtains. One curtain rises, and now we begin to perceive that some dancers are turning in place, some are moving across the stage together, some seem to be flying through the air. As the next curtain rises, and the swirl of colors and shadows resolves into a variety of bright costumes against colored lights. Another curtain and we become aware of the intricacy of the dancer's movements, the way some rise like angels into the beyond and others twirl with delight or stand transfixed . . . As yet more veils are lifted, more pieces fall into place, and yet the mystery persists . . . At last the final sheer curtain rises and we see the dancers without any distortion or obstruction, and the scene on the stage becomes the interior of a suburban shopping mall, with milling shoppers, kids chasing each other, girls showing off their new outfits, boys circling girls, and flights of dancers riding escalators. Think of this modern "Dance of the Seven Veils" as a metaphor for our human interactions; a constant shedding of layers of ignorance and misperception until we understand what's really happening.

Along the process of understanding, we observe other human beings through various filters; all human interactions are influenced by some degree of distortion or lack of information. Each layer adds its own qualities and colors to our perception, obscuring some details and distorting other details, obstructing a clear vision.

Among the many filters that veil the truth, the most prominent fall into three categories: perceptions, emotions, and cultures.

Perception

More efficient perception of reality and more comfortable relations with it.[52]—Abraham H. Maslow

Perception is not just about how we gather information from our environment through our cognitive senses, it's also about how we organize that information in our brains so it's available when it's needed to assure our survival and growth. How we organize that information in relationship to our previous experiences, as we encounter something we consider new, is based on emotions and feelings that change as an event unfolds. That information then becomes our reality.

In a sense, there is no fixed physical reality; there are only individuals' interpretations of it. Therefore, in any negotiation, it's imperative that we compare people's perception of the situation and examine how they arrived at their conclusions. Consider the two following scenarios.

The employees at Brandon Equipment in California were becoming upset and resentful toward Adam, a sales rep with thirty years on the job, who they'd noticed slipping out of the office every day an hour before five o'clock quitting time. Rumors spread that Adam was "late for his nap," that he was past his prime and being given "special treatment" by soft-hearted management.

During the annual performance reviews, Christine, an energetic young sales rep who was a stickler for management by the book, mentioned Adam's behavior to her boss, implying Adam's retirement was overdue. Her reality was clear.

Her boss pointed out to Christine some facts she was not aware of. He told her Adam's clients were largely on the East Coast, a three-hour time difference, so Adam routinely arrived at the office an hour or more before everyone else to make phone calls. What's more, at the end of the day it was Adam's habit to stop by the shipping center to double-check his clients' orders and make sure deliveries were on schedule. The way the boss saw it, Adam, far from being a drag on the department, had been putting in an extra hour every day for the past three years. And not one of his customers had had ever complained of unfulfilled orders or delays. The boss dreaded the thought of Adam retiring. He'd be impossible to replace.

Christine's attitude changed drastically after processing this "alternate" reality, and Adam soon became her role model and a source of inspiration.

In another case involving a business, Thomas, the manager of Alexander Gourmet Markets, an upscale purveyor of fine food and deli items, was upset with the quality of produce he was receiving from a supplier, GreenPack Fruits and Vegetables. He decided to call Michael, his account rep at GreenPack, to vent his frustration.

Thomas complained to Michael that, according to what the staff was reporting to Thomas, when a box of avocados or pears was opened the entire box was either entirely too ripe or entirely too green to appeal to shoppers. This was Thomas's reality, based on his knowledge of one side of an issue.

Michael was surprised, since GreenPack had worked out a system of painstakingly sorting produce (avocados and pears in particular) and numbering the shipping boxes to ensure they would be opened in order of ripeness. As they looked into the matter further, they discovered no one had explained this system to Alexander Gourmet's stocking staff, a situation Michael promised to rectify.

Here was a good example of a situation where two perceptions of reality were in conflict, but a fuller perception of the actual facts gave both parties a sense of relief, and the relationship between the two organizations quickly expanded.

In a negotiation, as parties proceed based on their positions of what they perceive to be the facts, it's essential to determine possible limitations of our sources of information and examine exactly how we arrived at conclusions based on the perceived facts of the situation.

In conflict-resolution negotiations in particular, examining and clarifying perceptions can play a very significant role, because many conflicts grow out of misunderstandings we haven't bothered to trace to their roots. In both case studies described above, once perceptions were compared and the facts clarified, perceived villains turned out to be heroes.

In our own everyday experiences in our families and work, we encounter different perceptions of the same situation. Two siblings can have very different perspectives on their parents. Two couples dining together at the same table in the same restaurant, even ordering the same entrees, can have vastly different experiences—"crisp and flavorful" versus "undercooked and gamey"; "lively ambiance" versus "crowded and noisy." Two investors looking at the same opportunity can have wildly different views about to its value.

Some years ago I had an enlightening experience that involved observing two perceptions of a situation. In 1998, the day after I had purchased a multi-unit property in La Jolla, California, I was standing in the street and overseeing the arborists clearing overgrown trees. A fellow investor walked by, who owned a number of apartment buildings in town, and with amazement pointed out to me that "a sucker had paid over a million and a half for this, can you believe it?" Inside of myself, I smiled without saying to him that I was the sucker. This was due to his perception of the value of the building as purely an apartment. What he did not know was that I had purchased that building so I could upgrade into condos (commonly knows as condo conversion). This property in particular caught my eye; I noticed that the rental units were being advertised as "condominium quality."

Exploring further into the history of the building, I discovered that it had been built originally as a luxury condo complex (generous parking and storage spaces, and top-quality materials and workmanship), but due to a combination of market conditions in 1988 and some minor design shortcomings, the original developer couldn't sell the units quickly and had been forced to rent them instead. The current owner listed it only as a typical apartment building. For me, converting those units into condos would entail far less expense than would other buildings in the same category. With the discovery of the property's hidden value, the building was in fact a bargain from my perspective—a very different perception.

Culture

If the doors of perception were cleansed everything would appear to man as it is, infinite.[53]—William Blake

Another "veil" that quite often colors our perception of a situation is cultural conditioning. The diversity of our distinct cultures adds much beauty, color, and nuance to our understanding of facts and events, but cultural differences can also generate ambiguity, unfamiliarity, and uncertainty when cultures collide.

When Saddam Hussein[54] was still the absolute ruler of Iraq, the US diplomat Bill Richardson was assigned the task of negotiating the release of two Americans being held in an Iraqi prison. Richardson recalls an important moment. The setting where this occurred was in the only conference room in one of Saddam's vast palaces and the man was not known for seeking others' opinions. Suddenly the dictator slammed his fist on the table and stormed out of the room with his delegation close on his heels. The meeting had been the culmination of weeks of preparation, and all the elements for an agreement had seemingly been in place, but at that moment all the careful work seemed to collapse into failure, while the lives of two Americans hung in the balance.

Shocked and bewildered, Richardson turned to his advisors for some explanation of what had just happened, and explained it this way:

They all shrugged. Searching for a clue as to what he did to piss off Sadam so badly that he reacted that way, but the best minds available could offer only shrugs at the dictator's mercurial behavior.

Desperate for a clue Bill turns to his interpreter. *What the hell is going on?*

The interpreter replied in a matter-of-fact-manner: *You crossed your legs.*

This was not getting any easier or clearer, so Bill asked: *So what?*

The interpreter explained: *You showed the bottom of your shoes and that is an insult in Arab culture.*[55]

The code of conduct and fundamental beliefs of a society, community, or organization, or of an ethnic, racial, socioeconomic, or religious group are "givens," expected behaviors of the group's members as they interact with one another. Since these behaviors represent longstanding traditions as well as shortcuts for smoothing the way forward, they are expected to be honored not only by the society's members but also by outsiders seeking acceptance. A very simple and genuine desire to learn about other cultures will go a long way, whether in Paris, Mumbai, or the Bronx.

As our global village becomes more and more interconnected, it behooves us to be mindful of the diverse codes of etiquette that various people honor. Indeed, in many modern societies—American, for one—ethnic and cultural diversity is so deeply knit into the fabric of society that tolerance and mutual respect are essential for even simple daily interactions. It's almost impossible to understand the details of every cultural group's practices and beliefs, but taking the time to gain at least basic knowledge goes a long way in demonstrating our respect for what we cannot hope to entirely fathom.

For enlightened negotiators, essential knowledge for those crossing cultural, lingual, and ethnic borders includes an appreciation of factors such as pace and timing, formality, and discretion, as well as commonly expected gestures of respect, and hierarchy.

THE PURPOSE AND PROCESS
OF NEGOTIATION

For the typical American, the goal line of a business negotiation is a signed deal, and since "time is money," the tendency is to get down to business as soon as possible. In many other cultures, however, signatures on a piece of paper are incidental compared to a sound underlying relationship, and the primary goal of the negotiation is to establish trust and understanding.

For Americans negotiating in cross-cultural situations, a practical approach that doesn't dishonor our own brisk and democratic cultural standards is to establish a rapport on a personal level quickly, a task at which Americans excel, and to make a genuine effort to get to know one's counterpart. Depending on the culture, the setting, or the issues ultimately at stake, this might require a few minutes, a few hours, a few days, or a lifetime of dedication and study.

Go with the flow. First find a common bond, build a sense of connectedness, acknowledge you have much to learn, and then move forward.

The Element of Time

Punctuality can be viewed as a spiritual as well as a practical virtue. Sensitivity to time, however, varies widely among different cultures and groups. Even among the pluralist cultures of the modern European Union, historically Germanic, Anglo Saxon, and Scandinavian cultures to the north are likely to have narrower interpretations of "on time" than, for example, Latin or Mediterranean cultures to the south. The international trains of the EU might share precise timetables, but the odds that passengers are settled in their seats when the conductor calls "All aboard!" varies significantly from one location to another.

Travelers through the Middle East often discover that rail schedules are an approximation, subject to other priorities, and in parts of Africa or the Asian subcontinent, trains arrive and depart when factors too complex to fully comprehend come into alignment—but trains are still considered "on time."

So here we have a quandary. Many spiritual teachers consider punctuality to be an expression of one's spiritual commitment, a fulfillment of a mini-agreement as a step in keeping a much deeper and broader promise. But as enlightened negotiators, we must also be sensitive to what might be vast differences in the perception of time in our counterparts, who might not yet be slaves to a clock as much as we are. The best policy is simply to honor the standards of one's own culture by being punctual and then showing flexibility toward others who define punctuality more loosely.

On the other hand, a person shouldn't be expected to wait forever. Patience and accommodation have their limits.

It's natural for cultures that have been around for millennia to perceive time on an exceptionally long scale, and Asian cultures in particular are legendary for their discipline in waiting for the auspicious moment. During the expansion of China's trade with the West it hasn't been uncommon for Western negotiators to be unnerved by the endless "hang time" of their Chinese counterparts.

Patience is a virtue, but testing others' patience isn't. Playing hard to get, showing up late or not at all, waiting until the eleventh hour to begin dealing in earnest. These are sometimes used as tactics to throw an opponent off balance or manipulate the flow of the process, perhaps to hold out for a better offer to materialize or resistance to wear thin.

If you find yourself noticing the first signs of foot-dragging or limits-testing tactics, at the very least, be prepared to extend your deadlines and wait-out long uncertainties.

Remember you also have every right to expect that your own cultural norms and civilities will be honored, and you might remind your counterpart that the train is pulling out of the station.

In a training session many years back, the response from the instructor to a question posed by one of the Fortune 500 presidents had a profound effect on my understanding of punctuality. The question was: "Why is it that no matter what I do and how early I plan for meetings I am always ten to fifteen minutes late?" The instructor responded loudly and clearly: "Because you think your time is more important than others' time!"

Formality or Informality

The style and tone of negotiation is set with the first words, and the first transaction is often an exchange of names. The level of formality of the first exchange often sets the atmosphere for everything that follows. Forms of address (names and titles), the dress code, the level of diction, and the range of freedom in using humor or sharing personal anecdotes depends on cultural background as well as the issues at stake.

Americans in general tend to observe fewer formalities than their counterparts from the United Kingdom (Americans abandoned powdered wigs immediately after gaining their independence from Britain) as well as other European or Asian nations with long traditions. English speakers often overlook the significance of formal versus familiar second-person pronouns in other languages; *vous* versus *tu* in French, for example is a distinction that most English speakers lost when *thee* and *thou* fell out of usage. The distinction requires a conscious step, an outward acknowledgement of acceptance, that the English avoid.

Americans and Australians tend to move quickly toward familiarity and informality, adopting a first-name (or even nickname) basis within the first few minutes, while people from Asia, the Middle East, and some Latin countries often need more than one session to feel comfortable setting aside titles and surnames. And in some cases, a person of high authority or advanced age would *never* be addressed with anything more familiar than "Sir."

For example, when Alexander, a young investment banker out to conquer the world like his namesake, secured a meeting with Sheikh

Abu Salah of the United Arab Emirates to discuss financing one of the largest real estate development contracts in the Middle East, he had visions of great things ahead.

When the appointed day came and Sheikh Abu Salah and his entourage were ushered into Alexander's conference room, they were quickly made to feel welcome by the Alexander's team. Throughout the morning, the delegates smiled warmly when Alexander offered his first name and shrugged off his concern that he was being too familiar.

An atmosphere of friendliness and ease settled over the room as coffee and refreshments were brought in and shared, and Alexander, knowing these were busy men and eager to make the best of the moment, began to outline his firm's proposal. The Sheikh's delegation listened attentively, took copious notes, and nodded approvingly as he went into detail for several hours.

Thrilled that the morning session had moved along so comfortably and eager to keep the momentum going, in a gush of good will, Alexander impulsively announced to the Sheikh, "Tell you what, I'm going to buy you all lunch!"

The UEA delegates fell silent, set down their pens, and chose the moment to arrange their sleeves. The Sheikh rose from his chair and spoke for the first time.

"You are buying *me* lunch?" he roared at Alexander. "I buy you! I buy your company! I buy your family!"

Sheik Abu Salah and his entourage marched out of Alexander's office. It was a harsh lesson for Alexander to learn that in Middle Eastern culture you may "invite" someone for a lunch, or they might be your "guest" for a lunch, but you only "buy" someone lunch if they cannot afford it themselves.

The prudent and respectful approach to negotiations with counterparts from more formal cultures is to begin formally and allow the time for your counterparts to settle into informality and familiarity at their own pace. Wait to be asked before you get down to business issues. Once a foundation of trust and understanding is in place, minor missteps are more likely to be forgiven.

EMOTIONS

When dealing with people, remember you are not dealing with creatures of logic, but creatures of emotion.[56]—Dale Carnegie

When something "stirs" our anger or compassion, when it "moves" us to weep or laugh, that's *emotion*. The word *motivation* shares the same Latin root, *movere*, but the two words connote very different concepts. When we're motivated, we are energized toward an intended goal. But if our movement lacks direction or intention, we might be in the grip of emotion, and the same added energy might only cause us to bump around aimlessly like jiggling atoms or fly off on a tangent. Emotions are difficult to keep under control. Enthusiasm and excitement can sometimes morph into stubbornness, compulsiveness, or fear, leading parties from their optimal course.

As we discussed in an earlier chapter, the Hierarchy of Needs is a useful visualization of what motivates us. Needs at the most basic level trigger innate emotions in us that move us toward satisfying that need by any means necessary.

A human being is a bundle of emotions: aspirations, desires, fears, insecurities, pride, joy, and countless others. Allies can evoke our emotions to lead us forward; foes can exploit them to lead us astray or put roadblocks in our way. In enlightened negotiation, mindfulness of your own emotions and those of other parties can be crucial in navigating toward your goal.

An Example of How Emotional Responses Can Affect a Negotiation

La Jolla Shores is a beachfront section of the quaint town of La Jolla, California, north of San Diego. In the early 1990s I was representing the owner of an oceanfront lot on a cliff with an expansive 270-degree view. I had helped him acquire the property for a million dollars in a distress sale, and now, only a year later, a buyer was willing to pay twice that for the lot.

The week before the thirty-day due diligence period was to end, which was two weeks from close of escrow, just as I was about to leave my office I answered a call from Helen, the agent representing the couple buying the lot.

She wanted to know if her clients could have two more weeks for due diligence. The request, this late in the process, came as an unpleasant surprise to me. Since we had already supplied all material facts the buyer had requested and there hadn't been any concerns or objections from her clients, I had assumed the transaction was going smoothly. Delaying the closing by two weeks represented a significant inconvenience for my client, who was eager to close swiftly and move on. I knew he had lined up a tentative investment with the proceeds of this transaction and didn't want to lose the opportunity.

Helen's call came at the end of a long and busy day for me, and the prospect of bad news wasn't welcome. In a worst-case scenario, Helen's call might be interpreted as an act of bad faith, the first sign that the terms agreed to in the negotiation were unraveling. If that were so, my client would want to know about it.

As we discussed earlier, the two weeks extension was a *position* and the issue was *time;* and I was eager to discover the *need* or the *interest* of her clients. So I asked her, "Why do your clients need another two weeks?"

Rather than giving me a direct answer, Helen reacted as if I'd questioned her integrity. "Why are you making a big deal about this?" she said.

Now with a new tone of voice I repeated my question. "Helen, *why* exactly do they need two weeks?"

"Hey, they're paying top dollar for this property," she replied. "Don't they deserve the benefit of the doubt and a simple two-week extension?"

In my mind, I was simply clarifying her client's needs, but I probably repeated my question more forcefully than I intended. "Helen could you *please* tell me what your clients are trying to do with two more weeks that they *weren't* able to do so far?"

Helen became defensive at my "demanding tone" and before long was telling me, "I can guarantee, if you're going to make a federal case out of this, the deal will be off."

I tried to tell her I was only clarifying the situation.

I could hear her voice shaking as she cut in, saying, "No you're not. You haven't even offered to ask your client if he's willing. It's not your client, it's *you*. You're being uncooperative and stubborn, and I don't deserve this."

She continued to lash out, "Do you think you can sell a vacant lot, in this market, at this price, in two weeks? You have buyers with two million dollars in their hands lined up around the corner?"

I was getting more frustrated and she was becoming more emotional by the second. In a moment of clarity I said, "Helen, it's late. One day won't make a difference. Let's take a break and talk about this first thing in the morning."

She agreed, and we hung up with as few words as possible.

The next morning when Helen called, there was a much different tone to her voice. She sounded like a different woman. She shared with me that her only daughter had left for college the morning before, and she hadn't realized the effect it would have on her. By the end of the day, all the tension she'd been feeling as this day had approached had been replaced by a sense of loss and suddenly being alone. And then she'd gotten a call from her clients in a panic, begging for more time. Helen apologized for having handled our conversation so poorly.

Helen explained that this deal was very important to her, partly because her clients sincerely wanted the location for the dream house they'd planned, and they were people she'd come to care about. The problem was that they'd suddenly realized their Los Angeles architect wasn't sure they could get approval from the city of San Diego to build a four-thousand-square-foot home on the lot. "You know all the restriction on ocean-front lots, all the government agencies involved," she said.

Something occurred to me. "Did you say four thousand square feet?" I asked.

"Yes, is it a problem?"

"Maybe not," I told her. "As I recall, the previous owner of the lot had plans for a *six* thousand square foot home, designed by a local architect. Why wouldn't their plan which is smaller be permitted?" I asked Helen to let me see what I could find out.

By late afternoon, we had both architects in a conference call, and the previous owner's architect confirmed the couple's dream house would be perfectly acceptable on my client's lot. Once that was clear, the need for a deadline extension disappeared.

In retrospect, it had been easy for me to perceive at the time that Helen was reacting emotionally during our first conversation, although I did not have a chance to find out why. Now I understood. Here was a woman facing the anxiety of separation from her only child, not to mention the pressure of coming up with college tuition. She had a fear of losing not just her commission, but the confidence of her clients as well, and was feeling insecure in her own self-image as a professional. She hadn't wanted to go into details simply because she didn't want to be seen as unable to hold a transaction together. Running up against an unreasonable broker on the other side was the last straw for her!

I was also getting frustrated with her elusive responses, when I remembered:

Speak when angry, and you make the best speech that you will ever regret.[57]—Groucho Marx

If it weren't for that moment of clarity when we realized we were in no shape to negotiate rationally, the transaction could easily have flown apart, leaving five people very disappointed.

The Power of Positive Emotions

Drawing upon positive emotions cultivates more cooperative frames of mind in the parties to a negotiation, facilitating agreement and a satisfying arrangement. Once positive feelings are exchanged, parties are more likely to reason through heuristics, mental shortcuts that lead us quickly toward positive outcomes. On the other hand, negative emotions flowing from distrust or an expectation of unfairness slow down the process by requiring increased levels of persuasion, explanation, and clarification for every step forward. As briefly mentioned in chapter 6, priming can be effective in planting the seeds of positive emotional motivation. Steven Neuberg in his study "Behavioral Implications of Information Presented Outside of Conscious Awareness"[58] found that exposure to certain emotional categories unconsciously activates related categories of knowledge that then influence our behavior or decision-making.

In one example, subjects who had been shown a movie about a mugger in action on city streets tended to react to a "stranger" (an actor employed by the researchers) bumping into them later on the street as an act of aggression and viewed it with concern. Subjects who had been shown a film featuring Inspector Clouseau (a hilariously uncoordinated French detective) reacted to an identical bumping encounter simply as amusing clumsiness.

In enlightened negotiation, priming our counterparts with positive observations or relevant past experiences can help orient them toward setting mutually beneficial goals and bargaining productively. In selling or leasing a dwelling unit, for example, sharing information about the neighborhood, access to public transit, parks, libraries, or a nearby farmers' markets can direct emotions toward visions of an enjoyable lifestyle that might later encourage agreement with the terms of the contract. If you're selling a car, mentioning its safety features to the parents of three children, or pointing out its sexy lines to a young driver, draws on emotions flowing from our basic need to protect our offspring or find a mate. If you're discussing your manuscript with a publisher, describing your own childhood experience of discovering the joy of books for the first time could remind the publisher of the emotional urges that led her into her career.

How to Deal With Emotions

Dr. Richard Davidson in his book, *The Emotional Life of Your Brain*,[59] outlines six dimensions of "Emotional Style." Each dimension is a continuum along which each person's characteristics are measured; the overall score determines one's personal Emotional Style.

The dimensions are:

> **Resilience:** Can you shake off a setback, or do you suffer a meltdown?
>
> **Outlook on life:** Do you have a positive or negative view of life in general?

Self-awareness: Are you aware of your own thoughts, feelings, and the messages your body sends you?

Social intuition: Are your sensitive to people's body language, tone of voice, and subtle messages?

Sensitivity to context: Are you attuned to the conventions of social interactions?

Attention and focus: Can you filter emotional and other distractions and stay focused on the subject at hand?

In the process of negotiation, awareness of these dimensions enables us to monitor the state of our emotions as well as those of our counterparts.

Self-awareness is perhaps the most important dimension you can develop for the purposes of enlightened negotiation. Through mindfulness practices and meditation, you can become more receptive to the inner messages of your body and more aware of how your emotions affect you. For example, you're able to notice changes in your breathing pattern. Are you holding your breath? If so, are you holding it after inhaling, or after exhaling? There's a difference: The former indicate a sense of danger, fear, or anger; the latter reflect sadness or loss. Are you breathing rapidly and shallowly from anxiety and fear, or slowly and deeply, in a calm and reflective state of mind? Do you notice any changes in your heart rate or perspiration? These are all forms of the body speaking to you, its language for expressing your emotional state.

The next question is how to deal with emotions.

Listening

As discussed in chapter 3, enlightened negotiation requires us to listen to our counterparts and convey to them that we are genuinely listening and we're empathetic. People need to be heard, need to voice our emotions. Once someone understands our emotions, we're better able to gauge their actual effect on the world and there's a good chance that the wild horse carrying us away can be tamed. Then all the energy can be diffused or channeled toward actions that might correct whatever's upsetting us. If from the outset of emotional expression there is no empathy and no listening, however, negativity escalates further and may erupt.

For example: Steve storms into Lisa's office where they have the following exchange:

> Steve: "We need to talk. Every time I mention our financial performance I feel I'm talking to a wall. We can't go on like this, Lisa, losing money month after month!"
>
> Lisa: "It's not that bad. I've looked at the financial reports. We're pretty much on track."
>
> Steve: "Lisa, you have your head in the sand! You can't go on ignoring this!"
>
> Lisa: "Me? I've been putting more time into our new promotion than I have on any project in my life, and I'm totally aware of what's at stake. For you to storm in here and accuse me of having my head in the sand is just . . ."

The escalating confrontation could go on for a long time along this destructive path, unless some intervention breaks the negative momentum and steers it back onto a constructive path.

For example: Here is Lisa's response:

> Lisa: "I hear how upset you are by the expenses, Steve. As your business partner, I have to say that it means a lot to me that you care so deeply about the success of our plans, and therefore I want you to understand that I share your concerns and I'm just as eager as you are to see us get through this rough period. We've been through challenges before, and we've always come through stronger and more determined. This is too important for both

of us to give in to our fears and never bother to pinpoint the source of the problem. We need to look at the figures together calmly and think through our options creatively. That's how we've always done our best work. Steve, can you free up some time after 2 o'clock so we can devote some attention to finding steps we can take?"

As a mediator I have listened to hours and hours of confrontational, emotional venting. Generally I acknowledge the feelings of each side and repeat the points of their concerns in terms of facts and figures, without emotional overlays. Then I watch the layers of emotion subside.

In a face-to-face negotiation, don't be afraid to take a break whenever you realize that emotions are rising, voices are getting louder, and tensions are building. In such situations, even a short pause or, if circumstances allow, a longer cooling-off period offers the parties a chance to reflect on their goals and adjust their attitudes.

Macro Vision

Highway 1 in Northern California is a beautiful drive. I feel so privileged just being on that road that I often envision myself being filmed by a camera far above me, taking in the expanse of the majestic setting, towering cliffs, and rugged coastline, the vast and glorious "big picture."

Taking in a larger scope can also be useful when the setting isn't quite so idyllic. When we're caught up in the heat of the moment and our emotions are boiling over, we have a tunnel-vision perception of reality, blurred by anxiety or unrealistic expectations, and patience and logic fall away. Standing back to consider the grand perspective can give us a new outlook on the situation at hand and can inspire us to set aside trivial issues.

An example of the benefit of having a big picture perspective is demonstrated by Jacob Tanzer, a former Associate Justice on the Oregon Supreme Court,[60] a wise mentor and a dear friend, who tells of a case in which he served as mediator in a dispute between two shipping companies:

> A major company headquartered in New York had brought a claim against a small Oregon-based contractor over a valuable cargo of industrial parts that had been damaged in transit.
>
> The owner of the New York company had come to the United States as a very poor young man with bold ambitions and had built a multinational empire. Normally, a dispute such as this would be resolved among anonymous lawyers and insurers, but for some reason the shipping tycoon had taken personal offense over the matter and insisted on a face-to-face confrontation with the owner of the Oregon firm. The contract between the two parties specified Oregon law and an Oregon arbitration forum for resolving any disputes; the tycoon and his team flew in from the East Coast by private jet and arrived by helicopter at the Portland hotel where the meetings would be held.
>
> The session opened in the usual routine manner of commercial mediation but was soon sidetracked by demands from the tycoon's team, clearly at his urging, meant to take control of the proceedings. I thought it best to separate the parties to their suites and talk with one group at a time.
>
> After two hours of shuttle fact-finding, it was clear to me the New York company's claim had weaknesses; indeed, the lawyers on both sides were well aware of this. The owner of the Oregon company knew the other side would be unlikely to win huge damage awards if the matter went to a local court, so there was no reason for him to offer a generous settlement at the outset.
>
> When I brought his initial low-ball figure to the claimant, the tycoon erupted in rage. "This is an insult!" he said. "I came all the way out here to settle this thing,

and that bastard isn't even serious enough to make a respectable offer. He thinks he can waste my time with this sideshow. Tell him I'll see him in court, and I don't care how long it takes or much it costs. It will be coming out of *his* pocket in the end."

The tycoon's lawyer held up the man's coat while he was slipped his arms into the sleeves. I knew that in another second, they'd both be out the door.

"Wait," I told them.

They turned toward me, and I knew I had to think of something to keep them in the room, though I didn't know what.

I said something pretty close to this: "Think about what's happening here. This is a business problem, and apparently you flew all the way out here to do what's best for your business. It's your business and it's your decision to make.

"Your business goal is to receive—without the delay, expense, and uncertainties of litigation—reasonable compensation for the *financial* damage you believe this party caused your company.

"If there's something *else* going on here, if that man has done something to offend your personal honor, is that relevant to the needs of your corporation? Whatever he might have done, it doesn't change or obviate your business goal in any way. It's simply a tactical problem for you to deal with, along the path to achieving your goal. So I suggest that you sit down and work with me to figure out a way to resolve this *business* dispute rationally and efficiently. After that, if you want to challenge him to a duel with sabers, you're free to do so."

The lawyer was taken aback at my bluntness with his notoriously proud and strong-willed client. For a moment it wasn't clear which way the tycoon would turn, but then he took off his coat and sat down, and nodded that he was ready to resume where we'd left off—with his opponent's seven-figure offer. He drew out his pen and wrote down an *eight*-figure counteroffer, at the high end of what would be reasonable, and sent me off with instructions to make clear to his counterpart that only another realistic offer in return would keep the process rolling. Anything short of that, and their next meeting would be in a courtroom.

I carried the message down the hallway to the other party, and added my own reminder that he, too, had come here to put the situation behind him rather than firing the starting gun for years of litigation. After giving it some thought, he sent me back with an offer that was at least within the ballpark. A few more exchanges ensued, a few more trips up and down the hallway, but a settlement was in place by lunchtime.

Reverse Your Thinking

When you are attuned to your emotions and can detect the first signs of their influence over your judgment, one way of bringing volatile feelings under control is to consciously *reverse* your thinking.

Let's say you've hired a landscape designer to improve the look of your home. You've taken the designer around your property, pointing out the details of what you have in mind—gravel here, a flowerbed by the front door, some plantings around a tree . . .

Weeks later the designer arrives with her plans, and as she spreads them out, you can't believe your eyes. You'd specifically said you want to get rid of a moss-covered statue at the far end of the garden, but she's planning to put the filthy thing outside the kitchen window! The front lawn has been replaced with a winding path through shrubbery! Instead of a flowerbed by the front door, the sketch shows a big rock!

Emotionally, you're at the first step of another winding path that begins with blurting out *This is the total waste of my time and money! Are you a moron?* and is likely to lead to unpleasantness. But instead of giving in to your first emotional impulse, you instead say, "I like it."

Now you have to think why that counter-intuitive statement might be true. Aside from the drawback that it ignores all of your preconceptions, what positive points *does* the plan offer? The designer explains that replacing the lawn with drought-tolerant shrubs will save $200 a month on water bills—*that's* certainly something to like. The more you think about it, the statue that has always looked so forlorn in the distance actually would be impressive if it were moved closer and framed by the arch of the kitchen window . . . And the big rock would certainly be an eye-catcher from the street.

Write a Venting Letter

There is a type of emotion that fills our minds with a stream of immaculately reasoned arguments expressed in our most eloquent words, and we hurry to capture these white-hot thoughts in writing.

Sometimes a concisely stated grievance (or even a love letter) actually can have lasting positive effects. Some of the most influential documents in human history, in fact, are essentially angry letters. The American Declaration of Independence, for example, is an open letter to the King of England, glowing with indignation and outrage, as well as key principles of human rights.

Abraham Lincoln is remembered as a great writer as well as a great leader, and yet his archives contain many letters he wrote as president but never sent. One famous example, a message he composed to an inept Union general who'd allowed Lee's army to escape, is factually accurate, well reasoned, Biblical in its eloquence, and also deeply emotional, ending, "Your golden opportunity is gone, and I am distressed immeasurably because of it."[61]

Yet Lincoln had the wisdom to realize the message probably wouldn't change the general's behavior for the better and certainly couldn't change what had happened. Once written, it had served its purpose without being sent, as a release valve for Lincoln's emotional "distress" and an outlet for what needed to be said, even if there was no one the lonely leader could say it to.

If emotion fills your consciousness with arguments and eloquence, it's often useful, in more ways than one, to channel that energy into getting it all down in writing. But if you're aware of the subtle ways emotions can affect your judgment, you will also have the wisdom to refrain, at least until tomorrow, from hitting the "send" button.

Humor

Humor can be effective in diverting an emotional uproar headed at us full steam. Laughter is an involuntary reflex, and it's impossible to laugh and be violently angry at the same time. Even a flicker of wit worth only a chuckle can do much to diffuse a tense situation and break a vicious cycle of negativity.

A few words of warning are in order, however, since most of us aren't gifted comics, and a sour joke can be destructive.

Professional stand-up comedians are skilled at timing and "reading the room," gauging how the audience will react. We should also be wise enough to use humor only if we're confident of our skills (preferably through practice), certain that the place and moment allows this level of informality, and we know the gesture won't be misinterpreted.

Negative Emotions

Generally, people come to a negotiation with a bias toward their own self-interest, valuing evidence that supports their position and discounting that which does not. The less opposing sides know about and understand each other, the more insistently this bias asserts itself.

Negative emotions like anger, fear, and distrust only escalate our natural tendency to be wary, causing us to reject opportunities for cooperation and to be drawn to retaliatory behavior. In an intensely partisan political environment, we're likely to see the opposing side's facts and arguments as distorted or "backwards," confirming what we believed or distrusted in the first place. Once this vicious cycle sets in, it's hard to break the negative momentum and reverse course.

Martin Nowak, a professor of biology and mathematics and director of the Program for Evolutionary Dynamics at Harvard University, in an experiment[62] using a variation of what's known as the "Ultimatum Game," studied our tendency to abandon self-interest and endure a loss just to punish the perceived "unfairness" of the other side.

The Ultimatum Game involves two parties. Player One receives a sum of money ($100) and must offer a portion of it to Player Two. If Player Two accepts, then both can keep the money. If Player Two refuses, then neither party keeps any money.

The economically rational presumption is that the second party will accept *any* offer, even if it were only one dollar, because it's still something rather than nothing. How much the other person stands to gain or fail to gain ought to be irrelevant.

In Nowak's experiments, however, more than fifty percent of subjects rejected offers less than thirty percent, the point at which they perceive distribution of the windfall so inequitable that they're willing to "pass" on the offer just to show disdain for it or to punish the first party for having made the offensive offer.

When our perceptions are distorted by spiteful emotions, even a free lunch can taste sour.

MINDFULNESS OF OUR SELF

Remember to remember!—Walt Baptiste

The three basic tenets of Zoroastrianism are simple yet profound: Good Thought, Good Word, and Good Deed. In practicing enlightened negotiation, it benefits us to pursue mindfulness of our intentions, mindfulness of our words, and mindfulness of our actions.

As evolved human beings, we should ask ourselves: Are our intentions, communications, knowledge-gathering, and creativity worthy of our evolved consciousness? Do our thinking, our speech, and our actions truly represent our core values and our higher Self?

In order to grow, fulfill our potential, and exceed ourselves in anything we must aim high; our dreams and imaginations must reach beyond our limits if we are to excel. Why not extend our reach by making use of the social fabric that surrounds us, through *connectedness*?

MINDFULNESS OF OTHERS

If you treat an individual as he is, he will remain how he is.
But if you treat him as if he were what he ought to be and
could be, he will become what he ought to be and could be.[63]

—Johann Wolfgang von Goethe

Namaste: In India and some other South East Asian countries, this is the word people use to greet each other. *Namaste* means "The divinity within me honors the divinity within you; the divine light within me honors the divine light within you."

A formal way to say hello in Austria is *Grüßgott* (pronounced "gruus got"), which translates as "salute to God." *Shalom* in Hebrew and *Salam* in Arabic mean "peace," that familiar state of inner security derived from completeness. The use of *shalom* in the scriptures always points toward a transcendent awareness of wholeness.

In the process of enlightened negotiation and in the spirit of co-creation, the concept of mindfulness acknowledges the divine presence we feel within us as well as its great potential for creation and prosperity generation at many levels. We need to recognize as well that we are human beings prone to mistakes, and therefore we must practice forgiveness.

In doing so, we are the guardians of divine potential. We recognize that some human beings are suffering from experiences and conditioning that stand in the way of achieving their full potential. Ego, greed, jealousy, false pride, and short sightedness cause them to betray trust, deviate from truth, and act without compassion. As the guardians of divine potential, we must not support or feed such wastes of divine energy.

Kirsten, a student from Germany, came to me after my class on enlightened negotiation and told me about a conversation she had with her parents the night before the class. Her parents were in the midst of a nasty divorce, and things had reached a crisis. Kristin, who loved them both, had been devastated by the news at first, but frankly it didn't come as a surprise. She shared with me that, as much as she ached to have the family stay together, it was obvious that the love her parents had felt in their youth and during their early years had faded now that that their children had moved away. They had simply grown apart in recent years. Living together was making neither of them happy.

The negotiation course, Kirsten told me, had given her a totally new perspective on how conflicts might be resolved and allowed her to see that the bitterness her parents were feeling indicated they were on the wrong track. Determined to help, Kirsten asked her parents to give her a month to work out an amicable settlement between them.

During the next week, she spoke with each parent individually, instructing them in the basics of enlightened negotiation and walking them through the process of exploring their separate and shared interests, coming up with options, then visualizing and co-creating solutions.

The process was an eye-opener for the parents. They saw the value of co-creating separate futures, just as they'd co-created a loving family and a prosperous business in the past. The fact that it was their little girl, rather than lawyers, who was maturely and lovingly guiding them made them both eager to learn more and focus on a harmonious settlement.

Toward the end of the semester, Kristin told me the most interesting part of the negotiation concerned the business her parents had built together, the major issue in dividing the material assets. Their lawyers assumed the only solution was for one parent to buy-out the other, or for both to sell the business to a third party or liquidate it for the assets.

In working through the enlightened negotiation process, however, it became clear to them that neither would be happy giving up their life's work. They realized they could still remain very valuable to one another as business partners while setting off on separate personal lives.

At the end of the course, Kristen stopped by to tell me her parents were looking forward optimistically to the rest of the long process of separating. After all, they would have to get along to continue their work. They were very grateful for the help she'd given them, which saved them a small fortune in lawyer fees—so grateful in fact, that they were setting aside that amount as an education fund for Kristen to pursue her PhD.

MINDFULNESS OF THE PROCESS

Mindfulness saves a lot of hassle.[64]—Sogyal Rinpoche

We should keep in mind that the process of negotiation is a dynamic endeavor flowing toward a common goal of co-creation. Like any dynamic process, it is subject to countless factors interacting and affecting its path toward completion.

We can picture the process of negotiation as a sport like football, where many forces are reacting to each other. The *process* is everything that happens between one whistle and another, between a start and a conclusion. Once each play begins, it sets a static formation into motion and becomes vectors and dynamics that everyone has to adapt to quickly. It has a momentum and a life cycle of its own, rising in an arc and then falling to a conclusion. New formations take shape and new patterns play out.

Much the same thing happens in the dynamics of dance partners getting to know each other, or jazz or comedy improv performances. In each case, there must be spontaneity, but there are also conventions to which the parties must adhere. The process grows like a vine, given constant nurturing and attention, from its inception to its flowering.

The key factors for a successful process include:

Momentum

Like any dynamic activity, each negotiation process has a momentum and a rhythm. It's essential to avoid losing momentum, especially over prolonged negotiations of days, weeks, or months. An agreement between a parent and child that the next report card must show improvement if there's going to be a camping vacation requires more than waiting to see what the next report card says; it requires constant monitoring and support, a gradual yet constant day-by-day improvement.

Finalizing the sale of a business is a similar situation: a succession of step-by-step tasks that must be completed—monitoring inventory, working with vendors and clients, transferring responsibility for orders and repairs, and executing a mountain of "sign here" paperwork. Without constant forward momentum, small complications can bring the process to a halt.

Resilience

As a dynamic activity, negotiation is likely to vary considerably from a planned course as it feels its way forward toward completion, and significant changes might be required long before the end is in sight. Change can be challenging.

In the examples above, what if a new teacher takes over the child's class, or a customer files a lawsuit during the stages of transfer of a business? What if a law is passed (or struck down by a court), affecting the licensing of that business? Such "plot twists" are good occasions to remember that the Chinese symbols for *challenge* and *opportunity* are identical. The event is whatever we choose to make of it.

In the late 1980s, United States International University, which had campuses in California, Great Britain, France, and Mexico, was seeking accreditation for its campus in Nairobi, Kenya, a country notorious at the time for bureaucratic processes that could become very long indeed if the system weren't "oiled" from time to time. Bribery and corruption were an accepted part of everyday life, and it wasn't long before the university faced opportunities to avoid endless delays in the accreditation process by paying the right people.

Dr. Gary Hays, the university's president, chose to stay focused on the school's principles and rejected outright any thought of an educational institution buying into a corruption system merely to expedite the process toward its expansion objectives. When in 1989 the University finally received its accreditation, its standing was strong and its reputation clean, and the degrees of its African graduates would be recognized around the world—this in itself became a great lesson for the school's staff. Through a challenging process, Dr. Hays' persistence and resiliency carried a vision through to completion.

Tenacity

Legendary football coach Vince Lombardi's motto, "Winners never quit and quitters never win," certainly applies to negotiation. Given the countless elements, in many cases, that must to come together in harmony for the process to succeed, tenacity is a valuable quality in a negotiator.

In my second year working in real estate, I had the opportunity to sell a 300-unit condominium project in San Diego.

The developer had defaulted on his loan and Interstate Bank had taken over the ownership. However, until the bank could find a buyer who would operate the complex, it retained the developer (headquartered in San Francisco) to handle marketing and sales of the units. The bank was eager to sell the entire project, but a new owner would bring an end to the developer's lucrative arrangement.

Since the bank was my client, I needed to work with the developer, communicating the terms of the new proposal to him and hopefully getting his response. He had no incentive to talk to me, of course, and he dodged my repeated phone calls over the next weeks, to the point that I was calling daily trying to catch him.

One day his assistant told me that he was "out of town." He was in San Diego, where I was, and I knew I had a chance of pinning him down. I immediately called his San Diego office, only to be told he was offsite at a meeting and would be back in two hours. When I called back two hours later, I was told I just missed him—he was on his way to the airport to catch his flight to San Francisco.

My entire office went on red alert to find some way to connect with this guy before he left town. Within twenty minutes, I was racing to the airport with a ticket for the seat next to him on the flight to San Francisco. For one and a half hours, I had his undivided attention.

A lot of persistence with a touch of creativity paid off!

Focus

Keeping our intentions and goals constantly in mind is the key to staying on track. We must also stay aware of our true nature and authentic motivations to navigate a true course.

More than seven billion people live on planet Earth, and for the most part things are working and running relatively smoothly. Somehow, billions of conflicting self-interests manage to align toward mutual benefit, and positive things get accomplished. Yes, there are pockets of violent conflict in the world, but we have the choice to instead support harmony and cooperation in our lives. What makes life beautiful is its diversity and energy, an infinity of atoms bouncing off each other and radiating color.

As humans, we must accept differences as a fact of our nature, but we can also be true to our essential connectedness. We'll never agree on *everything*, but we can be agreeable in our disagreements.

SUMMARIZING THE LAW OF MINDFULNESS

- Be mindful of your true nature as spiritual beings.
- Have awareness of what distorts your vision: Perception, Culture, and Emotions.
- Understand the power of positive emotion and how you can use it.
- Have awareness of the negative emotion in your interactions.
- Learn how to deal with emotions.
- Enhance your social intuition.
- Awaken the awareness of Self.
- Remain sensitive and stay aware of others.
- Be cognizant of the process.
- Practice resilience and tenacity.

8

The Law of Reflection

By three methods we may learn wisdom: first, by reflection,
which is the noblest; second, by imitation, which is the easiest;
and third, by experience, which is the most bitter.[65]—Confucius

The Kadampas were early Tibetan Buddhists known for their devotion to the principles of Dharma. They practiced righteous living: living every moment of the day aligned with universal, cosmic laws. Their simple life of farming, herding, and crafting and trading elegantly useful objects was enhanced by a unique practice.

The Kadampa carried with them a small bag of pebbles, some white and some black. As they began their day, every time they had a positive thought about someone, complemented someone, or performed an act of kindness, they would pick a white pebble from their bag and place it in their left pocket. With any negative thought toward anyone, any harsh word or act of violence—if there was any act of disrespect toward another living being—they would put a black pebble in their right pocket.

At the end of each day, just before they went to sleep, the Kadampa would empty their pockets and count the number of white and black pebbles. This was their way of measuring their daily progress along the path of righteous living. They strived toward the day when all the pebbles would be white.

LOOKING BACK

After we've reached the completion of a negotiation, as enlightened negotiators we should feel a duty to reflect on how the process unfolded and what progress has been made. Are the parties closer to their ultimate goals, or are they further away? No professional athlete ever goes to the next game without analyzing the performance of the previous game; like them, we must consciously capitalize on our areas of strength and give extra attention to our weakest areas. Like them, we must study and learn from our counterparts.

An enlightened approach to negotiation can benefit many other areas of your life. When you apply to your other waking moments what you've learned as a result of your experience, it can have a positive influence on your relationships with family members, acquaintances, neighbors . . . any situation requiring give-and-take among people.

A negotiation diary can be a useful ally in your quest toward the perfection of your skills. At the end of each significant negotiation, perhaps even at the end of each day, you can take inventory of positive accomplishments and setbacks, measure your progress in tuning your communications with others, and make note of areas in which you need to make more effort.

Recording your observations about the other side's skills and progress can also teach you a great deal. In the course of the day, what did your counterpart say or do that made you feel positive and more connected with them? Think about ways of expanding on that opening tomorrow. Was there something in their behavior that *wasn't* helpful? Resolve to *avoid* emulating that aspect of their performance.

One of my teachers, Walt Baptiste, always reminded me: *When someone wrongs you, don't demote them in your mind or be disappointed with them. Rather, resolve that you won't do the same.*

By what measures should you evaluate your practice of enlightened negotiation at the conclusion of an agreement? How about these:

- Are you better off?
- Is the other side better off?

- Have you made a positive contribution to the world around you?
- Could you have done this more intelligently?
- Have you maximized your resources?
- Are your relationships stronger?

Whatever measurements you use, it's essential to take time to reflect, review your performance, and evaluate the outcome.

It would be beneficial to pause and reflect on the following universal elements as they relate to your values, your ideals, and your interactions.

The following are some suggested types of reflections:

Prosperity

We think of prosperity as synonymous with success, fortune, abundance, and growth. The opposite end of the spectrum would be failure, poverty, loss, and decline.

Though prosperity is often associated with money and material assets, we shouldn't think of it narrowly.

A prosperous world is a better world, since a community whose members grow and prosper is aligned with humankind's true nature. We negotiate in order to succeed and enrich some area of our lives, whether it's health, family, happiness, relationships, career, or knowledge—Enrichment through negotiation doesn't necessarily mean a lucrative business deal. Western developed cultures emphasize the economics of prosperity, whereas in the Eastern traditions, collective and spiritual notions of prosperity are embraced.

The outcome of a negotiation should be measured by enrichment of our overall purposes and principles. As enlightened negotiators we should think of prosperity broadly and look beyond the outcome to its effects. Would we consider monetary gain alone a successful outcome if it also takes a significant toll on our health and family? Would launching a successful career be worth losing valued relationships? How do we measure a success? Despite the fact that we could pursue abundance in one, or in a few of these areas, the wise and intelligent approach to measuring prosperity is balanced abundance.

When prosperity becomes associated with mere opulence, we cross a line into acquisitiveness beyond our real needs. A greedy or glutinous measure of success takes over, a devouring hunger for things that never satisfy.

Walt Baptiste, who often talked about manifesting prosperity, always added the words "sufficient unto the need." It is this awareness that protects us from egotistic desire for more and more, and from being disconnected from our true nature.

Edward, a top-notch architect in Los Angeles, has countless stories about his encounters with the rich and famous.

He told me about an opportunity he'd once passed up, the chance to design a multimillion-dollar showplace residence for a professional athlete coming off a championship year. Money was no object, and the more spectacular and trend-setting the design, the better. An architect's dream commission.

The prospective client had recently broken up with his *domestic partner* (as architects record these things in their notes) and was on the cusp of a deep relationship with a new *associate*. But she proved to be, as the architect discovered in his first conference with his prospective clients, a *significant challenge*.

She challenged every iota of the design, and it was clear she was gifted in the theatrics of criticizing architecture.

Edward recalled, "In all my years as an architect, I've witnessed many arguments between partner-clients, and some of them have been toxic. But *this* woman pushed the envelope. I came out of every meeting physically exhausted and emotionally drained. Her objections and sarcastic put-downs were legion, but it all came down to establishing her own importance, as a way of solidifying her relationship with her new boyfriend.

"I felt for him," Edward told me. "He's a great athlete, a role model for the rest of us. Every time I met with them, I wanted to scream at this guy, *Wake up! Can't you see what she's doing to you?*

"With all the positive elements of this project—the fat commission, the great PR—any architect in my league would have assigned all the headaches to a subordinate and started pushing through orders for concrete.

"But for me, the challenge wasn't in getting the signature on the contract, but in whether I'd be compromising a lot of my principles and sacrificing my peace of mind."

Edward took a week to evaluate the situation, and at the end of that period of reflection surprised himself by deciding to walk away from the project.

"I told my prospective client that, although I was motived by my desire to help him create a comfortable home, the situation as it stood made it impossible for me to function as an architect.

"It just wasn't right," he told me.

That might have been the end of the story, but there was an enlightening postscript.

"The next year was a *lean* year, as the Bible says," Edward said. "My firm had to cope with a crash in the residential market. Commissions were scarce."

"And then, fresh off another championship, the athlete appeared at my office one day with a his *new* associate on his arm—a lovely young woman with a beautiful smile."

The commission would be more complicated this time, they admitted. The previous plans were half completed, and the blueprint was a mess, but they trusted his judgment.

"'Just make it livable,' the new girlfriend instructed me. 'Make us a home.'

"The design we came up with was featured in upscale magazines and won us a lot of contracts," Edward told me. "They're still living there," he added. "They have three kids now."

Infinity

When you look back over your performance, you should also take in a broad perspective that includes how the environment is now changed and the ripple effect of your actions on events in the future. You should look toward the horizon before you take the next step.

As discussed earlier, we should remember the symbolism of the numeral 8, associated in some cultures with prosperity. In many Asian cultures in particular, eight represents good fortune and is considered the most fortuitous of all numbers. The opening ceremony of the Summer Olympics in Beijing began on 8/8/08 at 8 seconds and 8 minutes past 8 p.m. local time.

In various cultures and wisdom traditions, the number 8 signifies perfect rhythm, felicity, and the state beyond time. In Christianity it signifies resurrection and regeneration.

In mathematics and science, the symbol for infinity is 8 turned on its side.

When does a negotiation end?

The symbolic act of signing an agreement is only a gesture; the performance and accomplishment of your agreement is the living essence of the negotiation. In many situations, the true significance of negotiation lies in the follow-through. Ultimately the effects of negotiation will linger far into the future. All the good and positive elements of your negotiation, as well as all the negative and less-than-desired actions, will have an effect on your future negotiations.

A deal may close, a case may reach a conclusion, but your reputation and how people feel about your part in putting the agreement together remains long after the ink dries on a contract. In addition to the vertical effect of getting something specific accomplished, there is also a horizontal effect, a broadening of possibilities for future development. Fair and compassionate treatment of a client or employee, for example, can have a wide impact horizontally as other customers hear of a pleasant experience with a manager or employees hear of a generous resolution of a dispute.

The congruity of one's actions with one's personal philosophy, or with the mission statement and core values of a business, will be judged by whether the roots we have planted bear fruit.

Karma

Karma means action. Karma, in simplest terms, is the law of cause and effect, both from an esoteric view and from a scientific perspective. It is the Newtonian law of motion, one should remember, that states that every action creates a reaction. Essentially, in our lives and our social interactions, *karma* means that our deeds, good or bad, will be reflected back to us at some point in the future.

Though the concept of karma is associated with Eastern religions, the New Testament of the Bible contains this Golden Rule: *So in everything, do to others what you would have them do to you, for this sums up the Law and the Prophets* (Matthew 7:12). The Bible also says: *Whatsoever a man soweth, that shall he also reap.* (Galatians 6)

Spiritual teachings, science, and our own experience agree: *What goes around comes around.* This is *natural* law, and we shouldn't expect to find a loophole.

The wheel of Karma advances through life; as you sow, so shall you reap. All your actions are the planting of seeds. All that is happening in your life right now is the result of what has been planted and taken root long ago, and whatever you are doing now sows the seeds of your own future and those of countless others.

Some of these actions you have undertaken consciously and some arise from *samskaras,* the latent impressions in your subconscious mind. These ghosts of past experiences can have a strong influence on your thoughts, expressing themselves through your speech and actions.

The good news is that, according to Eastern teachings, it is possible to mitigate karma, your actions of the past, and prevent undesired results in the future, just as Western religions recognize the power of atonement. Aspirants are advised to consider every act, no matter how trivial, a spiritual practice (*sadhana*) and meticulously examine their actions and the subsequent reactions in every situation life presents. It is through contemplation and meditation that you connect to your true essence and filter the influence of your latent impressions.

> Gayle Tauber, co-founder of the health-conscious Kashi food brand profiled in chapter 6, devoted much of her life to philanthropic endeavors after the sale of the company to Kellogg in 2000. She generously gave her time to many young women entrepreneurs, as well as to nonprofit organizations, and she was a welcome speaker before many organizations concerned about healthy lifestyles and preserving the environment. As her interests progressed, she contemplated becoming a professional speaker as a way of supporting and furthering the work she was doing.
>
> Out of the blue, she received a call from an association of industrial manufacturers wondering if she'd be interested in giving a keynote presentation at their annual conference in Ohio. Since the idea of charging for speeches was fresh in her mind, and since she hadn't fully worked out details, she asked for time to think about the offer, choosing to stay open to the proposal while she turned over in her mind the whole notion of speaking before commercial interests she couldn't be certain were aligned with her own.
>
> She asked herself whether, given her dedication to a holistic approach to business, she was the right choice for that type of organization. So she called Steve back, the association's representative who had contacted her, to make sure he knew who she was. He assured her they had researched her history and were thoroughly familiar with her accomplishments. Everyone on the committee had agreed that, yes, she was the right person for them.
>
> Steve made it clear they appreciated her making the effort to travel to the meeting, informing her that her flight and lodging would be taken care of.

The idea of leaving her warm La Jolla home to give a speech in the Midwest in November wasn't exactly inviting, but Gayle realized she already had an event in New York scheduled for that week. The manufacturers' conference could be a stop en route.

Since she had no idea what speakers charged for such things, she instead asked what they were prepared to offer her as a speaker's fee.

Steve immediately responded, "Does fifteen work for you?"

Gayle recalls, "At that moment, when I was analyzing the whole picture—taking into consideration that travel and lodging would be covered and that I had yet charged for a speaking engagement—fifteen hundred dollars seemed like a *very* good start."

She asked Steve to send her a copy of the agreement, as she wanted to confirm that his "fifteen" was the same as *her* "fifteen," and that she'd follow up with him in a day or two.

When the agreement came, Gayle was astonished to discover that Steve had meant fifteen *thousand* dollars. It was spelled out in words, so it probably wasn't a typo.

Now Gayle found herself confronted with an ethical dilemma.

In her mind, she had agreed to $1,500 in good faith, because she was satisfied she could give the association good value for that fee. If she blithely accepted the paperwork's terms, would it be ethical? Would she have to deliver *ten times* the performance she had planned, just to earn the fee on a karmic level?

What would you do?

As a seasoned business negotiator, Gayle realized that fifteen thousand had actually been Steve's *opening* offer, at the low end of what the association had budgeted for a speaker. Steve, she was certain, had done his homework and knew the market rate for keynote speakers. He probably was delighted that Gayle was accepting their first offer without asking for more.

Gayle realized that she was concerned about the karmic effects of accepting $15,000 when she'd authentically agreed to $1,500 . . . but she might be overlooking the larger scale of karma.

After reflection, it was clear to her that, for the work she'd been doing by contributing to her community—the countless individuals she'd already touched through the ripple effect of her efforts—a $13,500 windfall was the universe's way of balancing accounts, redeeming her contributions, and rewarding her goodwill.[66]

It was a manifestation of Universal support for further efforts. *Good karma.*

Generosity

Giving we receive, grasping we lose.[67]—Christian Smith

Generosity consciousness is a trait that makes the foundation of prosperity fertile.

Since generosity requires openness, it promotes a shift in consciousness or perception toward positivity, broadening, and infinite-focused thinking.

Generosity is sharing what you have with an open mind and heart, whether it be time, money, energy, food, a good story, a laugh, or support. His Holiness the Dalai Lama emphasizes that generosity isn't limited to material sacrifices but includes kindness, patience, and compassion.

Norman Wong, a contemporary "saint" who to many embodied devotion and righteous action, once shared a story of the days he spent following in his master's footsteps. They were walking together in the market square of a little village in El Salvador, shopping for the night's dinner.

His master stopped at the stand of a frail old woman displaying a few tomatoes and a handful of herbs. As the master picked up a tomato and examined its bruises, Norman pointed out to him, "The stand across the way has better looking tomatoes."

The master responded, "Yes, but she needs the money more."

When you stop to think about it, how much pleasure value is there in the difference between a glowing, luscious, ripe tomato and a slightly pitiful overripe tomato? Whatever the difference, we experience it in a flash.

But how much extended value is there in providing income for an impoverished woman?

As we peruse the world in a quest to satisfy our needs, could we be cognizant of the universal or cosmic environment in which we operate? Could we operate from our inner core and the authentic self?

Wisdom

Information, knowledge, and wisdom are very different entities. It has been said of the Internet era that there has never been a time when so many people know so little about so many things. We're flooded with data, awash in knowledge, and too often we equate "knowing everything" with acting wisely.

Wisdom is the judicious *application* of knowledge, our understanding of people, things, events, and situations. Wisdom is the ability to extract the essence of knowledge and act in a manner that is in harmony with universal principles.

King Solomon was known for his wisdom. God came to him in a dream and said: "Ask me for whatever you want and I shall grant it to you." King Solomon asked for wisdom and a discerning heart, which he received.

Two women came to the king for his judgment.

One of them said, "My lord. This woman and I live in the same house, and I had a baby while she was there with me. A few days after my child was born, this woman also had a baby. We were the only two in the house.

"During the night this woman's son died because she lay on him. Then she got up in the middle of the night and took my son from my side while I was asleep and put her dead son by my breast.

The next morning when I got up to nurse my son he was dead! But when I looked at him closely I realized that it wasn't the son I had borne."

The other woman screamed, "No that is a lie! This is my son; the dead one was yours."

But the first woman pleaded, "No! Yours is dead and this is my son." They argued before the king with no witnesses on either side.

The king reflected and then said to the women, "You both say, 'My son is alive and your son is dead,' so this is how we solve your problem. Then the king said, "Bring me a sword." He gave an order: "Cut the living child in two and give half to one and half to the other."

The true mother was deeply moved and sobbed: Please, my lord, give her the living baby! Don't kill him!" But the other said, "Neither I nor you shall have him. Cut him in two!"

Then the king gave his ruling: Love had spoken. "Give the living baby to the first woman. Do not kill him; she is his mother."

When all else failed, wise King Solomon reached for the power of love.

Love

As I write this, I wonder what someone picking up this book for the first time and opening to this section will think. What the heck is this book about? What does *love* have to do with skills in negotiation? Isn't negotiation about eat-or-be-eaten competition, jockeying for the slightest edge over an opponent, playing hardball?

Conventional wisdom places negotiation in a category of calculated, strategized, and rational behavior, whereas love is a passionate or compassionate irrational pursuit of our innate feelings and desires. There is little overlap between the two. If loves belongs in the category of the sacred, negotiation would belong in the category of the profane. The two seem mutually exclusive: We don't negotiate about matters of love, and love gets in the way of driving a hard bargain.

We love our children, our partner, our parents, our lover, our friends, and our heroes. We also love chocolate, flowers, ice cream, a song, a movie, a book, or a favorite poem. We use the term constantly, but what exactly do we mean by it? From the spiritual perspective, love is the essence of oneness; it is the experience of the moment in which the space between "you" and "me," "us" and "them," is dissolved and separation ceases. It is the expansion of our sense of self as it embraces and becomes integrated into a greater Self. Love is when the success and joy of another elates us just as if it were our own success and joy, and also when the hardships and sadness others experience makes us reach out with compassion.

In enlightened negotiation, mindfulness of that state of oneness enables you to feel connected and secure, not threatened. It establishes a framework for cooperation, opens you to new opportunities for mutual benefit, increases the efficiency of the process, and expands your relationships. Love has the power to motivate people, build bridges of understanding, and melt unyielding positions.

Keeping love out of negotiation misleads us away from our true nature and down a path of separation, competition, and blind self-interest. The myth that negotiation must be heartless only promotes the fallacy of zero-sum outcomes, dismissing the possibility that win-win outcomes also have validity. Myopic vision sets in; defensiveness and fear and greed surface.

Dr. V.S. Ramachandran, a neuroscientist at University of California, San Diego, points out in his book *The Tell-Tale Brain* that East Indian and Buddhist mystics believe there is no real difference between *self* and *other*, and that true enlightenment comes when we penetrate the illusory barrier separating the two. He says, "I used to think this was just well-intentioned mumbo-jumbo, but there is a neuron that doesn't know the difference between self and other. Are our brains uniquely hardwired for empathy and compassion?"[68]

Recent research in evolutionary biology and psychology has even found neural and possible genetic evidence of humankind's predisposition to cooperation. In addition, there is the physiological feature we discussed earlier: the oxytocin hormone that affects our ability to bond and feel a sense of belonging in a social group. Oxytocin was found to be present during interactions between a mother and a child, between lovers, and also in gatherings of people with a common purpose.

There are many legends and stories about the power of love, of its triumph and victory over the forces of darkness. Such stories resonate with us, and yet we treat them as fantasies or lore, not the sort of thing we experience in our everyday lives, in contemporary society. Border wars on the other side of the world, the value of the Euro, and celebrity scandals, on the other hand, seem somehow pertinent to our daily life.

Using the Power of Love in Negotiation

Between 2000 and 2008, the United States experienced an average of five mass shootings every year, according to the Justice Department. In 2013 there had already been twelve mass shootings by August 20, the date a gunman walked into a packed elementary school in a suburb of Atlanta armed with an AK-47.[69] He fired at the floor to make his presence known, and stormed into the office of Antoinette Tuff, the school's bookkeeper. If her instincts told her to try to get away or try to fight him off, she chose, instead, to *talk* to the troubled gunman in a loving way.

She connected with him by describing hard times she'd experienced in her own life. She told him she sympathized with him: "We all go through something in life . . . It's going to be all right, Sweetie." Antoinette let him know she'd been down the same road before herself, but she had picked herself up and was living a happier life now.

"I thought the same thing, you know, I tried to commit suicide last year after my husband of 33 years left me," she told the gunman. "I have a son with multiple disabilities."

An FBI hostage negotiator said her performance was a study in drawing a dangerous person back from the brink. At one point Tuff even told the gunman, "I just want you to know I love you, though, okay?"

Antoinette was eventually able to persuade the gunman to surrender, and there was one less massacre in a year plagued with shooting tragedies. She used no weapon, no tear gas, no threats or bluffs or deceptions. She armed herself only with the power of authentic love, compassion and sympathy. Once she was able to tap into that source of power, she had everything she needed to disarm a disturbed man with an AK-47. She didn't "outsmart" or "outplay" him; there was no calculated strategy guiding her method. Antoinette simply did what came naturally to her—feeling love for a suffering human being.

CONNECTING

Out beyond ideas of wrong doing and right doing, there is a field; I'll meet you there.[70]—Rumi

When people feel that they are valued or acknowledged, they tend to cooperate. On the other hand, when they don't feel valued, they have no motivation to contribute to a common purpose, and they become resistant to "submitting." If we're seeking another person's cooperation, we must *show* how much we value their ideas and guidance and effort. If we criticize, demand, and demean, what can we expect in return other than resistance and resentment?

We should be mindful that behind all the proposals and counterproposals and signed contracts, there are *people*. It's that awareness of the larger reality that makes it possible to reach agreements.

A good story demonstrating this is told by Bill Richardson, U.S. ambassador to the United Nations from 1997 to 1998, who earned the reputation of being a naturally gifted negotiator. He successfully put together agreements with some of the most notorious political figures of our time: two generations of North Korean leaders, Fidel Castro, and even Saddam Hussein. Presidents from both parties have called in his assistance in brokering agreements in some of the most challenging international environments imaginable.

At a World Affair Council meeting in the mid 1990s, I asked Mr. Richardson what someone should know to be a successful negotiator.

He started with a disclaimer, pointing out he had never received formal training in negotiation. "But I have an ability to connect with people," he admitted. "I like to connect with people. I've learned that even sworn enemies can strike an agreement if they treat each other like actual people."

In 1998, en route to Tokyo on a mission, Richardson asked his staff how the opening session conducted by his boss, Secretary of State Madeline Albright, had gone.[71] The news was disheartening: *Not well.* One staff member reported that Dr. Albright's Japanese counterpart had asked at the beginning of the session if it was all right to smoke, and she'd lectured him on the hazards of smoking tobacco and that he should consider quitting. The session had gone downhill from there.

At his first session with the Japanese delegation the next day, Richardson raised his hand with a question before they got down to business. "Mind if I smoke?" he asked, pulling out a cigar.

"You could feel the energy of the room shift," Richardson recalled.

He left Japan two days later with the assurances from Japan the State Department needed.

INTENTION

When Enlightened Negotiation reaches fruition, we have arrived at a new place, with a new level of understanding and consciousness. We've reached our destination, yet our infinite journey continues. The cycle of setting a goal and negotiating a path to it begins again. We have aligned the intention that we set at the beginning with the larger purposes in our life. We are inspired to reach further next time toward the overarching values that inspire ordinary people to extraordinary heights.

Negotiation can be an enlightening, even sacred practice—not in the sense of religious ideology, yet spiritual in the sense of operating in the world in a wakeful state of oneness. In that state, your everyday transactions embody your higher humanity, where you experience truth, beauty, goodness, love, and connectedness. In that state you receive guidance through your intuition and insight and you channel a flow of creative energy that empowers you to manifest your highest ideals.

If our personal lives, our professional lives, and our spiritual lives are not one, then how can we say we have a spiritual life?

May your inner light be your strength and guide.

SUMMARIZING THE LAW OF REFLECTION

- At the conclusion of negotiation take a moment to reflect on the areas of strength and areas that need to be strengthened.
- The result of negotiation has to be prosperous for you and for the other party.
- The deal ends but the results and reputations remain.
- How did you demonstrate generosity?
- How did you demonstrate love?

Endnotes

1 John F. Kennedy, Inaugural address, January 20, 1961, Washington, DC John F. Kennedy Library and Museum, Web.

2 Barbara Smith, "A Safe Place for Marriages," Latter Day Saints General Conference, October 1981. LDS Web.

3 Johann Wolfgang von Goethe, *Faust*, translation by Bayard Taylor (New York: The World Publishing Company), Public Domain, Kindle.

4 David K. Shipler, "Reagan and Gorbachev Sign Missile Treaty and Vow to Work for Greater Reductions," *New York Times*, December 9, 1987, Web.

5 *Tao Te Ching* Lao-tzu, *Annotated & Explained* (SkyLight Paths Publishing, 2006). www.Taoism.net.

6 Paul J. Zak, *The Moral Molecule* (New York: Dutton, 2012).

7 Jorge A. Baraza, Michael E. McCullough, Sheila Ahmadi, Paul J. Zak, "Oxytocin Infusion Increases Charitable Donations Regardless of Monetary Resources, Elsevier: *Hormones and Behavior* Volume 60, Issue 2, July 2011, pp. 148-151.

8 Steve Jobs, Stanford University, June 12, 2005, Commencement Speech. http://news.stanford.edu/news/2005/june15/jobs-061505.html.

9 Brad Tuttle, "Warren Buffett's Boring, Brilliant Wisdom," *Time*, March 1, 2010, Web August 14, 2015.

10 The Organization for Economic Cooperation and Development 2008 Survey of 30 Industrialized Countries: "Percentage of People Expressing a High Level of Trust in Others."

11 Linda Lyons, "Gallup Panel: People Can't Be Trusted," Gallup, September 27, 2005, Web August 24, 2015.

12 Bloomberg Business, September 21, 2015.

13 *New York Times*, September 23, 2015.

14 Lucius Seneca, Annaes Epistulae morales ad Lucilium, no. 71, sect. 3; trans. Philip Gaskell, *Landmarks in Classical Literature* (Chicago: Fitzroy Dearborn, 1999), p.151, 225.

15 Ralph Waldo Emerson, "Fate" in *The Conduct of Life* (Boston: Osgood & Company, 1871).

16 Hakwan Lau, et al., "Attention to Intention," *Science Magazine*, Feb 20, 2004, Web August 25, 2015.

17 Annat T. Katz, "Business Negotiations Served on a Sushi Platter," *Dialogues@Rutgers*,Volume 4, p. 56 December 12, 2011. Web August 25, 2015.

18 Raymond Cohen, "Language and Negotiation: A Middle East lexicon," *DIPLO* 2001, Web August 25, 2015.

19 Roger Fisher and Bill Ury, *Getting to Yes* (New York: Penguin, 1991).

20 William Hollingsworth Whyte, "Is Anybody Listening," *Fortune Magazine* (September 1950 Microfilm).

21 Jalal al-Din Rumi, *The Essential Rumi*, translated by Coleman Barks (New York: Harper Collins, 1995).

22 Richard E. Farson, Carl R. Rogers, "Active Listening," Excerpt from *Communicating in Business Today*, R.G. Newman, M.A. Danzinger, M. Cohen (eds.) (D.C.: Heath & Company, 1987), *Gordon International Training August* 25, 2015.

23 Glenn Llopis, "6 Ways Effective Listening Can Make You a Better Leader," *Forbes*, May 20, 2013, Web August 25, 2015.

24 Sylvia Porter, "Are You Listening? Really Hearing It All?" *The Pantograph*, November 14, 1979, Web August 25, 2015.

25 Ralph Nicholds, "The Struggle to be Human," Keynote Address International Listening Association, Atlanta, Georgia, February 17, 1980.

26 Dr. Brian Wansink, "Food Psychology Tip Sheet 2004," *Food Psychology Cornell University* 2004, Web August 25, 2015.

27 Swami Veda Bharati, *Silence* (Rishikesh India: SRSG Publications, 2007).

28 Personal email to author, Del Mar, California. June 23, 2013.

29 John Bartlett, *Barlett's Familiar Quotations*, 10th ed. 1919. Web, Bartleby.com, August 25, 2015.

30 Eliot, *The Rock*, (London: Faber & Faber, 1934).

31 Abraham Maslow, *Motivation and Personality: A Theory of Human Motivation, Second Edition*. (New York: Harper & Row, 1970).

32 Abraham Maslow, *A Theory of Human Motivation* (USA: Start Publishing, 2013) A. H. Maslow, Originally Published in *Psychological Review*, 1943.

33 Abraham Maslow, *A Theory of Human Motivation*.

34 Personal letter emailed to author, August 27, 2013.

35 Jalal al-Din Rumi, *The Essential Rumi New Expanded Edition*, translated by Coleman Barks (New York: Harper Collins, 2004).

36 Oliver Wendall Holmes, *The Autocrat of the Breakfast Table* Reprinted (Teddington: Echo Library, 2006).

37 John A. Byrne, "How Well Jack Welsh Runs GE," *Business Week*, June 8, 1998. Web, August 25, 2015.

38 Abraham Maslow, *The Psychology of Science: A Reconnaissance* Joanna (Cotler Books, 1966), Ann Kaplan 2002, Digital.

39 James Thurber, *My Life and Hard Times* (New York: Harper & Brother 1933).

40 George Bernard Shaw, *Back to Methuselah: In the Beginning, Bernard Shaw: Complete Plays and Prefaces*, Vol. II. (New York: Dodd, Mead & Co., 1963).

41 Aparna A. Labro and Vanessa M. Patrick, "Why Happiness Helps You See the Big Picture," *Journal of Consumer Research*: February 2009.

42 A. M Isen, A. S. Rosenzweig, and M.J. Young, "The Influence of Positive Affect on Clinical Problem Solving," *Medical Decision Making* 11: 221-27, 1991.

43 Shirli Kopelman, Ashleigh Shelby Rosette, and Leigh Thompson, "The Three Faces of Eve: Strategic Displays of Positive, Negative, and Neutral Emotion in Negotiations," *Research Gate* Web 9/2/2015.

44 Bloomberg Business, "Fel-Pro's Warm and Fuzzy Meets Federal Moguls Rough and Tumble," Web, January 1, 1998.

45 Beth Potier, "HBS's Teresa Amabile Tracks Creativity in the Wild," *Harvard Gazette*, Feb 10, 2005, Digital.

46 Robert Lee Hotz, "A Wandering Mind Heads Straight Toward Insight," *The Wall Street Journal*, June 19, 2009, Digital.

47 George Bernard Shaw, *Back to Methuselah: In the Beginning, Bernard Shaw: Complete Plays and Prefaces*, Vol. II, (New York: Dodd, Mead & Co. 1963), p. 6.

48 Dana Carney, Amy J.C. Cuddy, and Andy J. Yap, "Power Posing: Brief Nonverbal Displays Affect Neuroendocrine Levels and Risk Tolerance," *Pub Med*, September 20, 2010, Web 9/2/2015.

49 A personal letter emailed to author, August 23, 2015, La Jolla, California.

50 Alice Calaprice, *The New Quotable Einstein* (Princeton: Princeton University Press, 2005).

51 Bob Kelly, *Worth Repeating: More Than 5,000 Classic and Contemporary Quotes* (Grand Rapids: Kregel, 2003).

52 Abraham Maslow, *Motivation and Personality: A Theory of Human Motivation, Second Edition* (New York: Harper & Row, 1970).

53 Abraham Maslow, *Motivation and Personality: A Theory of Human Motivation, Second Edition.*

54 Bill Richardson, *How to Sweet-Talk a Shark* (New York: Rodale, 2013).

55 Bill Richardson, *How to Sweet-Talk a Shark.*

56 Dale Carnegie, *How to Win Friends and Influence People, Revised Edition* (New York: Simon and Schuster, 1981).

57 Eve Starr, Inside TV, *Greensboro Record*, November 3, 1954, *Greensboro Record Genealogy Bank,* August 25, 2015.

58 Steven Neuberg, "Behavioral Impact of Information Presented Outside of Conscious Awareness: The Effect of Subliminal Presentation of Trait Information on Behavior in the Prisoner's Dilemma Game." *Research Gate,* Web 9/2/2015.

59 Richard Davidson and Sharon Begley, *The Emotional Life of Your Brain* (New York: Hudson Press, 2012).

60 A personal letter email to author by Jacob Tanzer, Portland Oregon, December 8, 2013.

61 Howard Wilford Bell, *Letters and Addresses of Abraham Lincoln* (New York: The Trow Press, 1903).

62 Nowak, Martin, Page, Karen and Sigmund, Karl, "Fairness Versus Reason in the Ultimatum Game," Science Magazine Online, September 2000, Web August 25, 2015.

63 Johann Wolfgang Goethe, *Wilhelm Meisters Lehrjahre*, 1795/6. 8. book, 4th chapter, Natalie to Wilhelm, Forgotten Books, London.

64 Sandra Pawula, "Mindfulness Saves a Lot of Hassle," *What Meditation Really Is,* May 3, 2011, Web September 4, 2015.

65 Rev. James Wood, *Dictionary of Quotations* (London, New York: Frederick Warne & Co., 1899); Bartleby.com, 2012.

66 A personal letter by Gayle Tauber in email to author, La Jolla, California, August 23, 2015.

67 Christian Smith, and Hilary Davidson, *The Paradox of Generosity* (New York: Oxford University Press, 2014).

68 V.S. Ramachandra, *The Tell-Tale Brain* (New York: W.W. Norton & Company, 2012).

69 Marcy Heinz, "Terrifying Moments with School Gunman Unfold on 911 Call," recording CNN 22 August 2013, Web, 9/4/2015.

70 Jalal al-Din Rumi, *The Essential Rumi,* translated by Coleman Barks (New York: Harper Collins 1995).

71 Jodi Kantor, "Personal Touch for Richardson in Envoy Role," *New York Times,* December 21, 2007. Web, August 24, 2015.

Index

About the Author

For thirty years Dr. Mehrad Nazari has successfully merged the business, academia, and spiritual worlds to become an award-winning business leader in Southern California, professor of International Business Negotiation, and highly regarded meditation and yoga teacher. He holds a PhD in Leadership and Human Behavior and an MBA, and he has been guided by some of the great spiritual masters of our time. He is the founder of Enlightened Negotiation®, a consulting and training organization dedicated to transforming the way the world interacts and negotiates. He lives with his beloved wife, Michele Hébert, and their dog, Sophia, in La Jolla, California.

Join the Global Enlightened Negotiator Community

Go to www.EnlightenedNegotiation.com to join the conversation.

Please see Dr. Nazari on LinkedIn and follow the conversation on Facebook and Twitter.

Become an Enlightened Negotiator with Hands-On Training:

Attend Enlightened Negotiation® Trainings. Learn how to enhance your leadership skills and elevate your daily interactions and negotiations for more meaningful results. Bring Enlightened Negotiation® Training to your organization to transorm your workplace from within. Workshops are offered for a half-day, one day, or two days. The workshops will enable you to increase workplace engagement, team building, morale, and productivity.

Join the Enlightened Negotiation® Mastermind group for continued support, growth, and lasting results.

To book Dr. Nazari please email:
Events@EnlighenedNegotiation.com.